Machine Learning Concepts with Python and the Jupyter Notebook Environment

Using Tensorflow 2.0

Nikita Silaparasetty

Apress®

Machine Learning Concepts with Python and the Jupyter Notebook Environment: Using Tensorflow 2.0

Nikita Silaparasetty
Bangalore, India

ISBN-13 (pbk): 978-1-4842-5966-5   ISBN-13 (electronic): 978-1-4842-5967-2
https://doi.org/10.1007/978-1-4842-5967-2

Managing Director, Apress Media LLC: Welmoed Spahr
Acquisitions Editor: Aaron Black
Development Editor: James Markham
Coordinating Editor: Jessica Vakili

Distributed to the book trade worldwide by Springer Science + Business Media New York, 233 Spring Street, 6th Floor, New York, NY 10013. Phone 1-800-SPRINGER, fax (201) 348-4505, email orders-ny@springer-sbm.com, or visit www.springeronline.com. Apress Media, LLC is a California LLC and the sole member (owner) is Springer Science + Business Media Finance Inc (SSBM Finance Inc). SSBM Finance Inc is a **Delaware** corporation.

For information on translations, please e-mail booktranslations@springernature.com; for reprint, paperback, or audio rights, please e-mail bookpermissions@springernature.com.

Apress titles may be purchased in bulk for academic, corporate, or promotional use. eBook versions and licenses are also available for most titles. For more information, reference our Print and eBook Bulk Sales web page at http://www.apress.com/bulk-sales.

Any source code or other supplementary material referenced by the author in this book is available to readers on GitHub via the book's product page, located at www.apress.com/978-1-4842-5966-5. For more detailed information, please visit http://www.apress.com/source-code.

Printed on acid-free paper

Table of Contents

About the Author

Nikita Silaparasetty is a data scientist and an AI/deep-learning enthusiast specializing in statistics and mathematics. She is currently pursuing her Masters in Data Science at Liverpool Hope University. She is the head of the India-based "AI For Women" initiative, which aims to empower women in the field of artificial intelligence. She has strong experience programming using Jupyter Notebook and a deep enthusiasm for TensorFlow and the potential of machine learning. Through the book, she hopes to help readers become better at Python programming using TensorFlow 2.0 with the help of Jupyter Notebook, which can benefit them immensely in their machine learning journey.

About the Technical Reviewer

 **Mezgani Ali** is a Ph.D. student in artificial intelligence at Mohamed V University in Rabat, Morocco, and researcher at Native LABs, Inc. He likes technology, reading, and his little daughter, Ghita. His first program was a horoscope in Basic in 1993. He has done a lot of work on the infrastructure side in system engineering, software engineering, managed networks, and security.

Mezgani has worked for NIC France, Capgemini, and HP, and was part of the site reliability engineer's team that was responsible for keeping data center servers and customers' applications up and running. He is fanatical about Kubernetes, REST API, MySQL, and Scala, and is the creator of the functional and imperative programming language PASP.

Acknowledgments

"And whatever you do, in word or deed, do everything in the name of the Lord Jesus, giving thanks to God the Father through him."

—Colossians 3:17

First and foremost, I would like to thank God Almighty for giving me this amazing opportunity, and for helping me to successfully complete this book.

Next, I would like to thank my Dad, S. Mohan Kumar, my Mom, Agnes Shanthi Mohan, and my elder sister, Vinita, for being my constant support, help, and inspiration throughout this endeavour.

I'm also extremely grateful for the entire Apress team, who worked tirelessly and patiently to review my chapters, put forward their suggestions, and provide the necessary guidance that I needed, with the aim to make the final product truly enriching to its readers. Working with them has taught me so much.

Of course, I mustn't forget my friends, acquaintances, peers, well-wishers, and other people in my life who contributed in their own way, by praying for me, motivating me, guiding me, and even tolerating me when I seemed to be too busy for them.

Last, but not least, I'm grateful for the Internet, which played a major role in this entire process.

Introduction

I remember one day, when I was about 15, my little cousin had come over.
Being the good elder sister that I was, I spent time with her outside in the
garden, while all the adults were inside having a hearty conversation.
I soon found myself chasing after this active little 4 year old as she bustled
around, touching every little flower and inspecting every little creature.

At first, she carried this out as a silent activity, the only noise being her feet
as she ran across the grass. After a while, however, she could no longer contain
herself, and she began questioning me about each and every object and
phenomenon within her radius of sight. For a while, I felt thrilled that I was
old enough to answer these questions satisfactorily. This thrill was short-lived,
however, as she began delving deeper in her thirst to know more.

This lasted until my mom came outside and called us for dinner. As I
gratefully made my way back into the house, I came to two conclusions:

1. The human mind is brilliantly inquisitive

2. I'm not as smart as I thought I was

Now when we think about it, it's quite interesting to note that all that
we know to do, from counting the number of toes we have, to singing the
national anthem on key, to naming the planets in the Solar System, are all
skills that we have developed over time.

Were we born with these abilities?

No, of course not.

But we do have the ability to learn how to do all these things, with the
help of our brain which continuously learns and processes information.
The more we learn, the greater our knowledge. The greater our knowledge,
the more intelligent we are.

Not just human beings, but animals too. A dog can be trained to sit, roll over, and play dead, by teaching it that when it does these tasks correctly, it can earn a reward in the form of a tasty treat. By knowing how to perform these tasks, it is deemed to be an 'intelligent dog'.

So how do we learn new things?

One way of learning is through enquiring. When my cousin was asking questions about everything she saw, she was trying to obtain answers from what she saw as a reliable source. She knew that I already learned about all these things, and so I could give her the answers she needed.

Another way of learning is by observation. Before my cousin began asking me questions, she was observing everything. She noticed that the sky is blue while the grass is green, and the grasshopper hops about while the ant crawls alongs the ground. She was able to learn new things on her own, without having to ask anyone for help.

The more questions she asked and the more she observed, the more her knowledge increased.

It's quite fascinating, really, to think that just by learning, a being can become intelligent.

It is this intelligence that made the world what it is today. People grew in knowledge and made new discoveries which made daily life quicker and more efficient. This resulted in an increase in the number and variety of jobs available and skills required.

Soon, people began to develop new ideas and methods to perform various tasks. They managed to create objects that could automatically do certain things, like hammer a nail, tighten a screw, and so on. In other words, people created what we now call 'machines', which were made to simulate the actions of a person. These machines reduced the amount of manual labour needed, especially in the process of manufacturing. We now have machines that have taken over a lot of our work - Leaving us with more time and energy for the slightly more intellectual tasks, which these machines could not do, because even though we could make the machines perform specific actions, we could not get them to think in the way human beings do.

Now consider this… What if machines *could* think, and therefore, perform these intellectual tasks as well?

A Simple Example of Artificial Intelligence

Consider an email inbox. Earlier, it was just a regular interface through which we could carry out trivial tasks like reading, replying to, and deleting emails. Nowadays, we have much more advanced inboxes, with folders for 'Spam', 'Important', 'Other', etc. Our inboxes automatically detect if something is spam, and send it to the respective folder. They even detect if something is comparatively important, and send it to the 'Important' folder. All other emails go under the 'Other' folder.

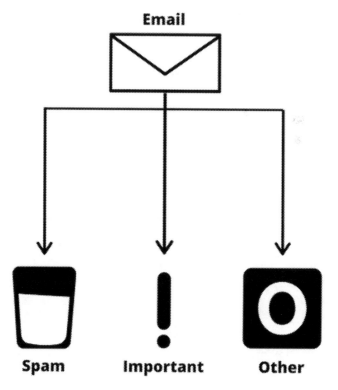

Figure I-1. *Email Classification*

But how does the inbox know the difference between these categories? The answer is simple - ***It learned***.

It learned how to detect if a message is spam, the same way we learned to do so - By looking for certain characteristics in the message. These characteristics include:

1. Irrelevant advertising

2. Request for sensitive information like an account number, contact information, etc.

3. Use of a general term to address the recipient, rather than using the actual name

4. Suspicious attachments

Once the inbox identifies such a message, it marks it as a possible spam email. It then sends that message to the 'Spam' folder. Thus, it saves us the trouble of dealing with numerous unnecessary emails everyday. All we need to do is go to our 'Spam' folder, select all the messages, and delete them. We don't even need to open the messages and read through them.

The ability of a machine to think and perform tasks like this is known as 'Artificial Intelligence' (AI), and the process by which it gains this Artificial Intelligence is known as 'Machine Learning' (ML).

This example of email segregation is just a simple application of Artificial Intelligence and Machine Learning. In fact, there is room for mistakes in this technology as well. However, these fields actually have massive potential. Just think about it - With the help of Artificial Intelligence and Machine Learning, we can create machines that think, infer, and then perform tasks. This would result in a quicker, more convenient lifestyle for people.

How?

Well, imagine a world where everything was automated, from picking our outfit in the morning based on the weather and the occasion, to driving to office through the busy traffic, to watering the garden at the right time. Our daily chores would no longer be ours to do. And, on a broader level, there would be even more applications, in the areas of business, medicine, education, and more. For example, there would be AI Recruiters, AI Doctors, AI Teachers, and so on. Long story short - People would be replaced by Robots that can do their work with greater efficiency.

Replacing Mankind with Machines

I think before we can consider replacing women and men with machines that can perform their work, we need to seriously ask ourselves the following question -

Would that be a good idea?

Well, at present, that's an inconclusive topic for debate. But it's definitely an interesting area to have a look at.

Some of the first AI bots started out as unbeatable champions in games like Checkers and Chess. These bots could replace a human player in games that require technique and strategy. This was not just an entertaining phenomenon to spectate, but also a measure of how advanced the AI technologies were. Seems pretty harmless, right? All the AI did was play a game really well.

Later, however, people realised that if AI bots could replace world class champions in games, then they can definitely be used in more cardinal situations. However, this did have its own drawbacks.

A very popular example of this is when *amazon.com Inc.* attempted to replace their human recruiters with AI recruiters. The results were not what was expected, as the machines became gender-biased and began rejecting applicants that were female. This caused quite a stir, as is expected, but also taught AI developers a valuable lesson when it comes to building self-learning machines.

Let's have a brief look at what happened.

The Gender-Biased AI Recruiter

In general, when a recruiter looks through a list of candidates for a job, what would be the factors that are considered? Some of them may include, in no particular order:

1. Relevant Experience

2. Area of Study

3. Qualification

4. Extra projects

5. Background

6. References

The recruiter would go through the resume, check their information with regards to the job that they are applying for, and probably give them a call to verify the information. Throw in a few extra tests and assessments as well, depending on the company. And if the person ends up being a good fit, they are given the job.

That's pretty much how an ethical employment process works, right?

Now when it comes to AI bots, they do not have the mind of a human being that enables them to understand the differences between relevant and irrelevant factors. All they have is data that they go through, find patterns in, and make decisions on.

The bots at this highly reputed company were trained with at least ten years' worth of job applications. And as we know, there are usually more men in the work-place than women, right? So the machine, while learning from its data, thought that a person's gender was an important factor to be considered when hiring. Its thought process was basically this:

Men = Good Fit,

Women = Bad Fit.

Thus, it began rejecting applications that had any sort of reference to females on it. In this way, it was biased against the female applicants.

Of course, the company made efforts to fix this. They altered their program so that it would remain neutral in such instances. However, many people are still quite critical towards it, as they feel that the machine can still come up with new ways to be discriminative.

This was a great learning experience for AI enthusiasts, because they realised that while all AI machines don't end up being prejudiced, it is still a possible outcome that needs to be tackled in the right way. It also shows that precaution must be taken while developing the AI machine itself. We must especially be careful about what kind of data we are using, since it is this data that the machine depends upon to learn.

It's quite interesting, isn't it? It's like raising a child. The child learns from all that she or he is taught. If she/he learns good things, and is given good experiences, it is more likely that the child will manifest it outwardly. However, if the child is raised with the wrong ideas, it will adversely affect her/him.

There have even been times when certain areas of Artificial Intelligence proved to be disappointing to researchers, and people nearly stopped showing enthusiasm towards the field. Such a period is known as an 'AI Winter', which we will read about later on.

One thing that almost everyone can agree on, though, is this: Artificial Intelligence and Machine Learning are progressing greatly, and are extremely important. If done in the right way, we can create systems that can truly revolutionise the world and the way we live.

This is why there is so much demand for jobs in these fields. This is also why there is so much research going on, and several new ideas being introduced with regards to it. Capturing data, storing it, and then programming with it has become so much easier and faster.

So as we begin our Artificial Intelligence and Machine Learning journey, let's have a look at some of the important concepts that we will need to know in order to really understand what we are getting into, and how we can use it to create useful and efficient technology.

PART I

Artificial Intelligence, Machine Learning, and Deep Learning

In Part I, you will be introduced to the fundamental concepts of artificial intelligence, machine learning, and deep learning. If you are a beginner, this will be a good way for you to get familiar with the terms and basics that are commonly used and good to know while working in this field. If you are a little more experienced, this will help you to recap all that you have learned so far. You might even come across something new!

What to expect from this part:

- An introduction to artificial intelligence

- An introduction to machine learning

- An overview of machine learning concepts

- An introduction to deep learning

- An overview of deep learning concepts

- A comparison between machine learning and deep learning

CHAPTER 1

An Overview of Artificial Intelligence

In this chapter, we will take our first steps into the world of artificial intelligence. Although it is a vast field, and we would probably require a whole other book to really dive deeply into it, we will go through a summary of important AI facts and concepts—what it is, how it came about, its benefits and drawbacks, and how it is being implemented in our present lives.

Artificial Intelligence Primer

We have all heard about intelligence. From experience, we have found that students who score higher grades supposedly have more intelligence than those who score lower. This may not always be the case, but it is what we tend to conclude.

We also know that Einstein had an IQ of about 160. What is astonishing is that a twelve-year-old girl in England ended up scoring 162, thus beating the world-renowned genius in this measure of intelligence.

So, what exactly is intelligence?

© Nikita Silaparasetty 2020
N. Silaparasetty, *Machine Learning Concepts with Python and the Jupyter Notebook Environment*, https://doi.org/10.1007/978-1-4842-5967-2_1

Intelligence can be defined as the ability to acquire and apply knowledge and skills.

This is why we are given an education from childhood. Over the years, we are fed with knowledge that is meant to help us become more intelligent.

Over the years, people worked hard and expanded their research and scientific advancements. They used their "natural intelligence" to come up with bigger and better innovations. Eventually, they were able to program machines to work and think like them, which they soon began to refer to as "artificial intelligence."

Artificial intelligence can be defined as the ability of a machine to think like a human being, in order to perform a particular task, without being explicitly programmed.

It is also sometimes referred to as "machine intelligence" and can be compared to "human intelligence." It is, as a matter of fact, inspired by a human being's natural intelligence. It aims to replicate the cognitive abilities of the human brain, like learning, understanding, and solving problems.

The Inception of Artificial Intelligence

Artificial intelligence did not always exist. It was probably only something that existed in people's imaginations, and maybe just an exciting part of a science fiction novel. However, around the late 1930s, people slowly began considering the possibility of machines' being able to think in the way that human beings do, which is what inspired researchers to go about making this a reality.

1930s–1940s: Over the Years

A few scientists from different fields came together to discuss the possibility and practicality of creating machines that could think and respond and act like human beings.

One of the early works that inspired machine learning was the Bombe machine made by Alan Turing and his team during World War II. This machine could crack the Enigma code used by the Germans to send encrypted messages. This was a major milestone in the field of machine learning.

1950s: Discoveries and Breakthroughs

In 1950, Alan Turing published a paper, "Computing Machinery and Intelligence," while he worked at the University of Manchester. In this paper, he introduced what is known as the Turing Test. In this test, he proposed that if a person is allowed to talk to another person and a machine, and if the first person is not able to differentiate between his two conversation partners, then the machine exhibits intelligent behavior. The conversation would be text-based only. This test proved to be a way to convince many people that a thinking machine was at least possible.

In 1951, Christopher Strachey developed a checkers program with the help of the Ferranti Mark 1 machine. Dietrich Prinz wrote one for chess as well. These technologies come under the "Game AI" umbrella, which is used even to this day to understand how far AI has come.

Around 1955, Allen Newell and Herbert A. Simon came up with the "Logic Theorist." It was the first program that was made for automated reasoning, and is thus known as the first artificial intelligence program. It ended up proving thirty-eight out of fifty-two theorems in *Principia Mathematica* by Alfred North Whitehead and Bertrand Russell, and thus opened the eyes of researchers to the possibilities of manipulating symbols, which could help with human thought.

In 1956, Marvin Minsky, John McCarthy, Claude Shannon, and Nathan Rochester organized the Dartmouth Conference. It was here that the term *artificial intelligence* was first coined by John McCarthy and accepted by researchers in the field. AI also gained a proper identity in the field of science during this conference.

1960s–1970s: Advanced AI

After this, interest in artificial intelligence began to grow rapidly. It was the hot topic at the time, and people were coming up with newer ideas and better techniques to help machines think. In the 1960s, researchers began developing robots as well. The WABOT project began in Japan in 1967, with an objective to create the first "intelligent" humanoid robot .

1970s–1980s: The First AI Winter

The 1970s started out pretty well for AI. The WABOT-1 was finally completed in 1972. It had limbs that could move either to move around or to grasp onto objects. It had artificial eyes and ears that helped it measure depth and direction. It also had an artificial mouth with which it could communicate with people in Japanese.

However, AI had still not reached the extent that people had hoped it would. Development seemed to go at a snail's pace, and investors were not satisfied with the situation. Eventually, they began to halt all funding for undirected AI research.

Some of the reasons for the slow rate at which AI was moving forward include the following:

1. **Need for massive data and storage:** Machines did not have the capacity to gather and store information about the world. This was a huge obstacle because machines require immense quantities of information in order to become intelligent.

2. **Need for greater computational power:** Machines still did not have the power to carry out any substantial computations.

3. **Need for more computational time:** Many real-world problems can only be solved with the availability of time, which is what was missing then. So, people felt that AI would perhaps not be able to provide any solutions for realistic issues.

Many critics also began stepping up against the field. They pointed out the lack of resources, unfulfilled objectives, and the unknown future of AI. By 1974, it had become extremely difficult to obtain funding for AI-related studies.

This resulted in many people feeling that artificial intelligence was not only a futuristic fantasy, but also an unattainable goal. The overall coldness in the attitude of people toward AI led to the first "AI winter," which lasted from 1974 to 1980.

1980s–early 1990s: The Revival and the Second AI Winter

In the 1980s, things started looking brighter for AI. People started implementing expert systems in their businesses, which is a form of AI programming that answers questions and solves problems within a particular area of knowledge. This led to a shift in focus in AI research toward knowledge engineering and knowledge-based research (KBR).

It was at this time that the Japanese Ministry of International Trade and Industry made the decision to invest $850 million in the fifth-generation computer project. Through this project, they wanted to create machines that could reason, converse, translate languages, and comprehend images.

Connectionism made a comeback as a result of the Hopfield Net, which is a type of neural network that worked differently but provided appreciable results.

In 1987, however, all enthusiasm toward AI abruptly decreased because of the introduction of desktop computers by Apple and IBM, which were less expensive and much more powerful. This resulted in a collapse in the demand for AI hardware. Expert systems were also found to be too expensive to maintain and improve.

Funding was stopped, and research was dropped. This led to the second AI winter, which went on from 1987 to 1993.

Late 1990s: AI Reborn

In the late 1990s, artificial intelligence once again became a topic of interest. Companies began to take up AI as their focus, and many AI technologies were being implemented. Funding for AI began once again, enabling AI researchers to move forward and develop newer and better inventions. A lot of goals were finally met, which motivated researchers to move forward in their work.

In 1997, IBM finished development of Deep Blue, which was the first computer to defeat Garry Kasparov, the world famous chess champion, which it did on May 11. The event was broadcast live over the internet, sparking the interest of millions of people. This was a huge milestone in the AI realm, as it demonstrated the vast potential that existed in training machines.

The reason for this was said to be the increase in the capacity and speed of computer processing. In fact, Deep Blue was found to be 10 million times faster than the Ferranti Mark 1. Over the years, technology improved, thus paving the way for better AI machines.

By 2000, there was still some skepticism toward AI. HAL 9000, a fictional AI character created in 1968, was based on the hope that similar AI technology would soon be possible by 2001. Unfortunately, this ended up being an unachieved dream, much to the disappointment of many researchers.

This did not stop them, however, and they continued working hard and investing time, money, and effort into the field. In 2005, a Stanford Robot was developed that drove autonomously for close to 131 miles on an unfamiliar desert route. Around 2007, a team from CMU created a vehicle that autonomously navigated 55 miles while following all traffic regulations. In February 2011, IBM debuted Watson, which defeated two *Jeopardy* champions, thus winning the quiz game.

Artificial intelligence soon branched out into big data, Internet of Things (IoT), data science, machine learning, and deep learning. People realized the need to specialize in a particular sector so as to collectively contribute to the advancement of AI.

As of 2020, artificial intelligence continues to be one of the most in-demand areas of employment and research, with people encouraging more and more innovative ideas to be developed and implemented, not just on a professional or specialized level, but also in our day-to-day lives.

Quick Bite   There are five Founding Fathers of artificial intelligence: John McCarthy, Alan Turing, Marvin Minsky, Allen Newell, and Herbert A. Simon.

Pros and Cons of Artificial Intelligence

Since its advent, artificial intelligence has been highly favored by some and highly criticized by others. It has its benefits, and it also has its drawbacks. Let's go through some of them to get a better idea of how AI has affected the world so far.

The Pros

Artificial intelligence became vastly popular mainly for the following reasons:

1. It allowed machines to replace manpower in performing certain tasks, especially mundane and tiring ones.

2.   It allowed machines to become much more efficient, giving them the ability to solve problems on their own and requiring less work on the part of developers.

3.   It can be accessed and utilized at any time.

4.   It can also perform tasks that would generally be difficult or dangerous for human beings to do.

5.   When developed well, there is less scope of errors on their part.

The Cons

Over the years, as artificial intelligence continued to garner people's interest, it also began to display certain drawbacks, including the following:

1.   It was expensive to develop and maintain.

2.   It resulted in unemployment, since machines began to take over tasks that people used to do.

3.   Many people misused the technology for personal benefit and unethical gain.

4.   At times it was difficult to find people with enough experience to develop the programs needed for the problem.

5.   It took a lot of time and computational power to develop the various AI models.

Challenges Faced by Artificial Intelligence

Keeping the pros and cons in mind, we can now understand that although artificial intelligence has deeply interested many people, it also struggles in many ways to reach its full potential. At present, the challenges faced by AI include the following:

1. The scope of artificial intelligence is somewhat limited. This is mainly because of the amount of resources, technology, funds, and manpower available for it.

2. Real-world implementation is still not easy. Many AI machines exist only theoretically or as prototypes, but have not yet been put into practical applications.

3. Security is a big issue when it comes to artificial intelligence. This is because AI requires loads of data in order to be trained, and this data can be taken either ethically or unethically from people. As mentioned before, AI ethics is a growing area of importance in the field of AI, but it still has a long way to go before it can really have any kind of significant impact.

Apart from the challenges listed here, artificial intelligence has also undergone seasons of disinterest. This has happened twice so far, starting in around 1974. It resulted in many AI developments' being stalled, and people's heading into other fields of work and research.

The AI Winter

As you have already read in an earlier section, there were times during the history of artificial intelligence when people's overall interest in the area became cold. To a certain extent, people nearly gave up on the field. They restricted the quantity of resources and funding given for its research and growth. Such a period is known as an AI winter.

The First AI Winter (1974–1980)

The first AI winter can be traced back to around 1974. It was not an abrupt break in the progress of artificial intelligence. Rather, it was an inevitable consequence of certain setbacks that occurred prior to it.

1. Around 1967, the "quiet decade of machine translation" began, where researchers found it difficult to correctly translate languages with the help of artificial intelligence. After spending enormous amounts of money in this area, the funding was finally stopped.

2. Approximately two years later, Minsky and Papert published their book, *Perceptrons*. This book explicitly critiqued perceptrons, which had a negative impact on connectionism. People soon abandoned the connectionism approach for years.

3. In 1969, the Mansfield Amendment was passed, as a result of which the Defense Advanced Research Projects Agency (DARPA) restricted their funding to projects that focused on military benefits only.

4. In 1973, the "Lighthill Report" was published, which evaluated the progress made and emphasized the downfall of artificial intelligence. Although this report faced plenty of public criticism, it eventually caused a feeling of pessimism to sweep over researchers and investors, who ultimately withdrew from the field.

5. In 1974, DARPA discontinued funding the Speech Understanding Research (SUR) program at Carnegie Mellon University, due to the latter's production of an inefficient speech-recognition AI machine that did not fulfill their requirements.

6. Thus, by 1974, the first AI winter had begun, mainly due to the lack of funding, which stalled any further research. Thankfully, this period only lasted until about 1980.

The Second AI Winter (1987–1993)

The second AI winter can be traced back to around 1987.

1. In the 1980s, LISP machines were invented, which were special hardware systems that were used for AI programming in the LISP language. However, by 1987, better alternatives were introduced, which reduced the demand for exclusive LISP machines. Later, in the 1990s, expert systems such as the LISP machine were found to be difficult to maintain. This caused a fall in their production.

2. In 1981, a project was started by the Japanese Ministry of International Trade and Industry to develop a high-tech reasoning machine. It was called the Fifth-Generation Project. In 1983, DARPA once again began to fund AI research. However, in 1987, the funding was again stopped. The team involved in the project soon found that their list of objectives for the project had not been achieved even after ten years. Decades passed with no results.

3. By the end of 1993, more than 300 AI companies had either been acquired, shut down, or gone bankrupt, marking the occurrence of the second AI winter.

Quick Bite   Following the second AI winter, many researchers and businesses avoided the term *artificial intelligence*, as they felt it had a negative aura to it. They thus began to use other names instead, including the now popular *machine learning*.

There is also plenty of research going on in the field of AI ethics, which is another important sector within the realm of artificial intelligence.

AI Ethics

The field of AI ethics is mainly concerned with the moral behavior and intentions involved in the development and implementation of an AI system. So, why are AI ethics important? To answer this question, let's consider the following two scenarios.

Scenario 1: Deepfakes

With recent developments in AI technology, systems can now create exact virtual replicas of actual people. These are known as deepfakes, where, for example, a fake video of a person can be created with the help of AI.

Now, obviously, this kind of technology can have various outcomes—some positive and some negative. This is where AI ethics come in to play.

Suppose a group of AI developers want to design deepfake videos of the president of their country. AI ethics make each of these developers ask themselves the question: Why am I doing this?

If the developer's answer is not selfish, harmful, or fatal, then they can proceed with what they were doing. However, if their answer is any of the above, then they may have to reconsider the motives behind their project.

Of course, in some cases, it is easy to decide whether an AI tool is alright or not. The problem is, sometimes it is not exactly possible to figure that out.

Scenario 2: Making Decisions

Most of us have already heard about self-driving cars, right? These cars are trained, with AI, to accelerate, maneuver, and brake, all while taking a rider to their destination.

There have also been videos online about these cars safely avoiding animals on the road, thus saving the life of the animal as well as that of the person inside.

But what if the car is in a situation where a crash is inevitable? And this time, it doesn't involve an animal, but another human being? What should the car do?

To have a better idea of this, let's take the following example:

A young father of four children is traveling in his self-driving car, returning home after a long day of work. The car is moving at a constant high velocity along a highway. Suddenly, out of nowhere, an old couple starts crossing the road, right in front of the car. The car now has two options:

1. It can swerve away from the couple, crash into the low cement wall on the side of the highway, and thus likely result in the death of the passenger.

2. It can save the passenger's life by crashing into the old couple, thus likely taking their lives.

What should the car do in this situation?

Some may argue that the car should save the old couple because that would be two lives saved, which is greater than the one life that would be lost within the car. Others, however, may argue that the young man still has so much to do in this world, and on top of that, he has his wife and children depending on him, and so it would be better to save his life.

This is quite a dilemma, isn't it?

Human beings themselves find it difficult to come up with a definite answer for this. However, we do have something that machines do not have, i.e., our natural instinct, which, in a way, helps us to make decisions in such situations. Machines need some kind of factual information to be able to differentiate between right and wrong. Thus, it would be difficult for the car to know what to do in such a case.

That's why AI ethics is a growing field in the world of artificial intelligence. Through discussions, research, and trials, ethical problems such as these can be tackled.

Once a solution is developed, however, new inventions and ideas can be implemented into our daily lives. Self-driving cars will no longer be a potential hazard. Deepfakes can be created for beneficial purposes. More technologies will come up, and there will be less fear in the hearts of people regarding what kind of developments are being made in the artificial intelligence sector.

Artificial Intelligence and IoT

The Internet of Things (IoT) is the connection of various objects in order to form a network of devices that can interact with one another. It was developed in order to enable non-living, unrelated objects to work together, assess their surroundings, understand a situation, and react accordingly, without the need for human intervention. IoT devices are interconnected with the help of software, sensors, and other such technologies. They send signals to each other, receive signals from one another, and thus exchange data via the internet.

Many researchers have begun integrating it with artificial intelligence. This has led to a variety of new technologies and devices that they soon hope to integrate into an average person's day-to-day life.

Applications of IoT

IoT has been greatly accepted and highly demanded due to its great scope in terms of usability. Some of its applications are discussed in the following sections.

Smart Homes

Smart homes refer to the phenomenon of home automation, where the home does tasks on its own, without the need for anyone to control it. So far, smart homes have been able to do the following:

1. Switch lights on or off.

2. Keep a check on the overall temperature of the home.

3. Make sure all electronic devices are turned off when not in use.

4. Monitor the health of the inhabitants of the home.

Smart homes aim to make life a little more convenient for people by reducing the amount of time or effort they need to put into little everyday tasks. They also aim to provide assistance to those who might be differently abled, and even to the elderly.

Wearables

Wearables, as the name suggests, are devices that can be worn and that collect data about the wearer for further processing. Some common wearables are as follows:

1. Heart-rate monitors

2. Fitness monitors

3. Glucose monitors

They also include smartwatches that can connect to a person's phone and interact with it.

Smart Greenhouse

The greenhouse farming technique aims to enhance crop yield by moderating temperature parameters. The problem is, this becomes difficult when it is required to be done by people. Smart greenhouses, therefore, can be used to fix this.

1. Its sensors can measure the various parameters.

2. It sends this data to the cloud, which processes this information.

3. An appropriate action is taken with regards to the plant/s involved.

This concept helps to reduce the costs of salaries and maintenance, and to increase productivity.

How Does AI Relate to IoT?

Artificial intelligence is a rapidly growing field of technology that has slowly begun to be incorporated into our lives to increase productivity, efficiency, and profits. IoT has also begun to be implemented in our daily lives with the help of faster connectivity and greater computational ability.

When AI and IoT are combined, we can obtain some powerful technologies that can be used to solve many worldwide problems and improve the way we live. AI and IoT can be integrated together to achieve greater outputs.

For example, in smart homes, artificial intelligence can be used to gather the data, analyze it, and then make the most suitable decision based on the information it has received.

Similarly, in wearables, AI can be used to collect, analyze, and process the data taken from the wearer in order to help the device respond in the right way.

Smart greenhouses can also use AI to monitor the conditions of the environment, alter them, and thus ensure that the plants receive the most optimal growing conditions.

Many researchers have agreed that artificial intelligence is the next step in the IoT sphere. It is true that the quantity of time, work, resources, and funds required for this will be a bit of a challenge, but considering the incredible amount of benefits such an endeavor would have, the investment would be worth it.

Summary

We now know what artificial intelligence is and how it has progressed over the years. We have studied its strengths and weaknesses, its challenges, and how we can make it more ethical and secure. We have even seen how to implement it with other useful technologies for maximum benefits. We can thus move ahead to some of the specifics of artificial intelligence—mainly, how to make a machine intelligent in order to use it in the real world.

CHAPTER 2

An Overview of Machine Learning

Artificial intelligence sounds pretty interesting, doesn't it? It's exciting to create a thinking machine that can do whatever you need it to do. And you don't need to worry about learning something new and extravagant—all you need to do is learn to program.

How convenient is that?

So, what exactly do you need to program? The answer is pretty straightforward: program the machine to learn! How else would it be able to think? This concept comes under the umbrella of machine learning, which is an extremely important part of artificial intelligence. Let's dive into it and see what it's all about.

What Is Machine Learning?

If the name isn't already a pretty obvious giveaway, here is a simple definition that should help you understand what exactly you are getting into.

Machine learning can be defined as the process of teaching a machine to think like a human being in order to perform a particular task, without being explicitly programmed.

Think about the first time you learned to read. You began by learning the alphabet, then you formed words by joining these letters together.

© Nikita Silaparasetty 2020
N. Silaparasetty, *Machine Learning Concepts with Python
and the Jupyter Notebook Environment*, https://doi.org/10.1007/978-1-4842-5967-2_2

Finally, you began to learn how to pronounce these different combinations of letters. And as you kept practicing, you became better at reading.

Machine learning works in the same way. The machine learns, understands, and thinks like a human being, and then uses this thought process to do some work. With machine learning, machines can be taught to perform higher-level tasks.

Just like human beings need to learn to increase their natural intelligence, machines need to learn to increase their artificial intelligence. This is why machine learning is so important when it comes to developing artificially intelligent systems.

The Machine Learning Workflow

A typical machine learning problem follows these steps:

1. **Defining the problem:** We first need to determine what exactly our problem is before we can begin solving it. We need to figure out what the problem is, whether it is feasible to use machine learning to solve it, and so on.

2. **Collecting the data:** We then need to gather our data based on our problem definition. The data is extremely important, and must thus be collected with care. We need to make sure that we have data corresponding to all the necessary factors required for our analysis.

3. **Pre-processing the data:** We need to clean up the data to make it more usable. This includes removing outliers, handling missing information, and so on. This is done to decrease the possibility of obtaining errors from our analysis.

4. **Developing the model:** We can now create our machine learning model, which will be used in solving the problem. This model takes the data as input, performs computations on it, then produces some output from it.

5. **Evaluating the model:** The model needs to be evaluated to verify its accuracy and to make sure that it can work on any new data that may be provided to it.

As we have seen in this workflow, machine learning is done with the help of data—loads and loads of data. Machines take this data, analyze it, and develop conclusions from it. This is how the idea of data science evolved to be an integral part of machine learning.

What Is Data Science?

Data science allows us to obtain knowledge from data.

The entire process of collecting, manipulating, analyzing, and developing inferences from data is known as data science.

Data science is, then, the combination of statistics, mathematics, computer programming, complex problem solving, data capturing, and working with data to cleanse it, prepare it, and use it.

The data that is obtained from the process of data science can, once it is prepared, be fed into a machine in order to help it learn.

Branches of Data Science

Data science consists of the following main areas:

- **Data collection:** Gathering the data

- **Data storage:** Keeping the data for later access

- **Data wrangling/munging:** Cleaning up the raw data for easier utilization

- **Data visualization:** Viewing the data graphically

There are two other areas, namely, big data and data analytics, that, although treated as separate entities, also deal with data and thus come under the data science umbrella.

Big Data

Big data refers to the storage of huge volumes of data. This data is mainly characterized in the following three ways:

- **High volume:** This refers to the quantity of data that is generated and stored. The amount of this data is immense as it finds its sources in images, videos, audios, and text.

- **High velocity:** This refers to the speed at which the data is generated and processed. Usually, this data is available in real time, which means it is continuously produced and handled.

- **High veracity:** This refers to the quality of the data. The data produced here can greatly vary, and this can affect the overall analysis.

Big data can be applied in the following areas:

- Communication

- Finance

- Retail

- Education

- Media

Some of the challenges that big data faces include the following:

- **Gathering data:** Since the amount of data is so huge, it is not an easy task to collect it.

- **Storing data:** Very powerful storage units are required to store such massive amounts of data.

- **Transferring and sharing data:** In order to successfully transfer and share large quantities of data, advanced techniques and tools are required.

Data Analytics

Raw data can be analyzed to observe trends and to come up with conclusions based on these trends. Thus, *data analytics refers to the inspection of data in order to derive insights and develop inferences and conclusions based on it.*

It follows several steps and consists of various methods that help in making the process more effective and in obtaining the desired results. It makes use of a variety of statistical and mathematical techniques.

There are four main types of data analytics, as follows:

1. **Descriptive analytics:** This is used to explain what has occurred. For example, it can be used to describe the present performance of a company.

2. **Prescriptive analytics:** This is used to predict what will occur in the future. For example, it can be used to determine the profits of a company based on its previous performance.

3. **Diagnostic analytics:** This is used to determine why something has occurred. For example, it can be used to understand why a company might be seeing losses.

4. **Prescriptive analytics:** This is used to figure out what needs to occur, i.e., what needs to be done. For example, it can be used to come up with better strategies and ideas to help a company get back on track and make profits again.

Data analytics can be applied in the following areas:

- Healthcare

- Energy management

- Travel

- Finance

Big data and data analytics are each very intricate parts of data science, and thus there is a huge demand for them, especially when it comes to employment. The data obtained as a result of these methods can then be used in machine learning and related fields.

There are various sources from which data can be obtained, depending on the use case. In the next section, we will go through some of the important methods that are used for data collection.

Collection of Data

Data is nothing but facts and figures that, when gathered together, produce some piece of information. This data can come from a number of sources, including the following:

1. **Surveys:** These are used to gather data from several respondents in order to develop a conclusion that can be applied on a broader scale. For example, studying the effect of social media on students in a particular school to figure out how social media affects school students in general.

2. **Polls:** These are used to understand people's opinions or sentiments toward a particular topic. For example, online shops can ask their customers for their opinion on the product they have purchased, and this information can be used to strategize better sales tactics.

3. **Interviews:** These are structured conversations in which one person (or group of persons) asks questions, while the other person (or group of persons) answers the questions. For example, news reporters interview a group of people at a protest to understand what they are protesting against and how the situation can be improved.

4. **Observation:** As the name suggests, this is the process of observing or watching the natural reaction, response, or behavior of the objects of study in order to come up with some useful inference. For example, observing tigers in their natural habitat can help wildlife researchers understand their needs so as to figure out how to better preserve the species.

Another way to collect data is simply by observing people, actions, or phenomenon. For example, we can use previous weather patterns to predict future weather patterns, or we can predict the outcome of an election just by observing the response that people have towards a particular candidate.

Data can also be collected from online sources, since there is so much content available on the internet nowadays. Some examples include gathering data from social media sites, scraping the web, or even just downloading datasets from online. One thing to keep in mind, however, is that before we use this data, we need to ensure that it is permissible and ethical to use.

Once the data is collected, it needs to be pre-processed before it can be used for any further applications.

Pre-processing Data

The data that we collect can have errors, missing values, extra information, and so on. This can cause problems in our machine learning process. Thus, the data needs to go through a type of cleansing, which is known as pre-processing.

Data Cleaning

The data is cleaned in the following ways:

- Removing data that is inaccurate, irrelevant, or incomplete.

- Transforming data to ensure they are of the same type or format.

- Checking if the data is acceptable for use.

Filling in Missing Values

Values can be missing for reasons such as the following:

1. Random error

2. Systematic error

3. Human error

4. Incorrect sensor readings

These values are dealt with in the following ways:

1. Removing the section that contains the missing data, as long as there is enough data left for the machine learning process.

2. Removing the attribute that consists of the problematic data or data that is consistent or can correlate with another attribute.

3. Assigning a special value like "N/A" for data that is missing due to acceptable reasons (for example, if a person fails to attend a match, their opinion of the match is invalid).

4. Estimating the missing value by taking the average value of the attribute.

5. Predicting the value from its predecessors.

Removing Outliers

An outlier is an irregularity within a set of values that varies tremendously from the rest. It can greatly affect the results of any kind of computation done on the set of values. A very simple example is shown in Table 2-1.

Table 2-1. *Outlier Computation*

	a	b	c	d	e	f	g	h	i	j
X	2	3	1	1	4	3	5	100	5	2

As we can see, the value for *h* is 100. This is much larger than the rest of the values, which fall within the range of 1 to 5.

In the same way, such irregular values can occur in data that is collected for data science purposes. These values need to be handled carefully to prevent inaccuracies or mistakes in our results.

The most commonly used method of handling outliers is to use data visualization to plot the data on a graph, after which irregularities are detected and then dealt with.

Transforming and Reducing Data

Data transformation is also known as data wrangling or data munging. It converts the data into a format that is readable to the machine learning algorithm. The data also becomes easier to learn, and a more accurate output can be achieved.

Data reduction removes certain attributes that are less likely to have a positive effect on the machine learning algorithm's outcome. For example, some attributes may have random values, values with very low variance, or a large number of missing values. In such cases, that attribute can be entirely removed from the dataset.

Types of Data

The data that is collected and used can be either of the following:

- **Labeled:** Each class/type is labeled based on certain characteristics so that the machine can easily identify and separate the data into its respective groups. For example, if you have a collection of pictures that are separated and tagged as "cat" or "fish" accordingly.

- **Unlabeled:** Each class/type is not labeled, and so the machine needs to figure out how many classes are there and which item belongs where, and then it must separate the data on its own. For example, if you have a set of pictures, but they are not separated and tagged as "cat" or "fish" accordingly. In this case, the machine would need to identify some particular features that differentiate one animal from the other (like a cat's whiskers or a fish's fins).

Based on the *kind* of data being used, there are two main types of machine learning methods:

- **Supervised learning:** This method uses labeled data.

- **Unsupervised learning:** This method uses unlabeled data.

Table 2-2 lists how they differ from each other.

Table 2-2. *Supervised/Unsupervised Learning Differences*

Supervised Learning	Unsupervised Learning
It uses data that is labeled.	It uses data that is unlabeled.
It does not require excess data for accuracy.	It requires excess data for accuracy.
Computational complexity is less, i.e., it is simpler.	Computational complexity is greater, i.e., it is less simple.
It does not find patterns on its own from a dataset.	It finds patterns on its own from a given dataset.

Each type of learning method has various types of algorithms that can be used to solve a machine learning problem. Let's take a look at some important ones.

Supervised Learning Algorithms

The goal of every supervised learning algorithm is to map the input to the output, as shown in the following equation:

$y = f(x)$

There are several algorithms that can be used to solve a machine learning problem with the help of supervised learning. These algorithms can be segregated into the following categories:

1. **Regression algorithms:** These algorithms contain outputs that are real or countable. For example, height (4 feet, 5 feet, 6 feet), age (27, 31, 65), or price (100 rupees, 20 pounds, 10 dollars)

2. **Classification algorithms:** These algorithms contain outputs that are abstract or categorical. For example, colors (orange, purple, turquoise), emotions (happy, sad, angry), or gender (girl, boy).

To give you some idea of what these algorithms are, let's go through three common types of algorithms that are used:

- Linear regression
- Logistic regression
- K-Nearest neighbors

Linear Regression

As the name suggests, linear regression is a type of regression algorithm. It models the relationship between a dependent variable and an independent variable. Graphically, it looks something like Figure 2-1.

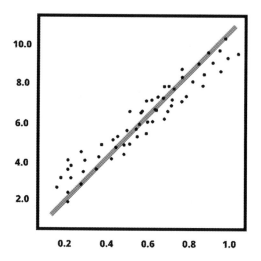

Figure 2-1. *Linear regression algorithm*

Logistic Regression

Although the name says *regression,* this is generally used as a classification algorithm. It is usually the first choice for programmers who wish to conduct binary classification. It looks something like Figure 2-2.

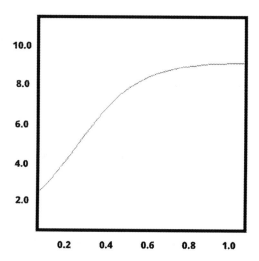

Figure 2-2. *Classification algorithm*

K-Nearest Neighbors

This algorithm can be used for both regression and classification. It assumes that similar units exist in close proximity to one another. It uses this idea to come up with a solution. It looks something like Figure 2-3.

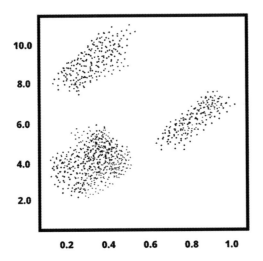

Figure 2-3. *K-nearest neighbor algorithm*

Applications of Supervised Learning Algorithms

1. **Spam detection:** Remember the very first email segregation example that we read about? This is done with the help of supervised learning.

2. **Bioinformatics:** This is the method of keeping a record of a person's biological information for later use. One of the most common examples of this is the security system on our cell phones, which can scan our fingerprint and grant us access accordingly.

Unsupervised Learning Algorithms

The goal of unsupervised learning algorithms is to discover possible patterns from the set of data that is provided. The algorithm has no prior information about the patterns and labels present in the data.

There are several algorithms that can be used to solve a machine learning problem with the help of unsupervised learning. These algorithms can be segregated into the following categories:

- **Cluster analysis:** This approach finds similarities among the data and then groups the common data together in clusters.

- **Dimensionality reduction:** This approach attempts to reduce the complexity of data while still keeping the data relevant.

Let us now have a look at two common algorithms that are used for unsupervised learning: K-means clustering and principal component analysis.

K-Means Clustering

The K-means clustering method forms k clusters out of a total of n observations. Each observation will be a part of the cluster with the closest mean. It looks something like Figure 2-4.

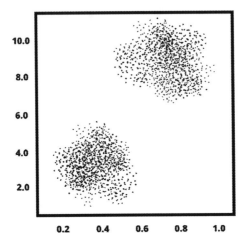

Figure 2-4. *K-means clustering algorithm*

Principal Component Analysis

Principal component analysis uses orthogonal transformation to statistically transform a set of potentially correlated variables to a set of linearly uncorrelated variables, known as principal components. It is used to reduce the dimensionality of the data. It looks something like Figure 2-5.

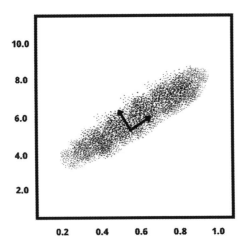

Figure 2-5. *Principal component analysis algorithm*

Applications of Unsupervised Machine Learning Algorithms

Anomaly detection is the identification of certain anomalies or observations that are different from the rest of the observations. These anomalies are also called outliers. For example, credit card fraud can be discovered by detecting unusual transactions made with the credit card.

Association is the process of identifying associations between different observations with the help of provided data. For example, in e-commerce it is easy to figure out the type of products a customer might be interested in by analyzing previous purchases.

Task Time Do a little more research on machine learning algorithms. You can even compare them with each other, as this will broaden your understanding of these algorithms to help you decide which one to use for any future projects you might have.

Apart from supervised and unsupervised machine learning, there are also two lesser-known methods of machine learning, as follows:

- **Semi-supervised learning:** This method uses some labeled data and a larger proportion of unlabeled data for training.

- **Reinforcement learning:** This method is similar to training a pet. It sends positive signals to the machine when it gives the desired output, to let it know that it is right and to help it learn better. Similarly, it sends negative signals to a machine if it provides an incorrect output.

Applications of Machine Learning

Over the years, as machine learning began to grow in popularity, enthusiasts began to do more research into different ways of solving machine learning problems. They soon came up with different types of algorithms that prove to be the most efficient, depending on the data and parameters that you are using. Thus, these algorithms became available for worldwide use. Developers can easily choose which method they want to implement and follow the algorithm accordingly.

Machine learning models are structured differently, based on what is required of them. We will go a little deeper into the architecture of a machine learning model later on in this book.

Now that we have some basic idea of what exactly machine learning is, let's take a look at some of its present real-world uses, as follows:

- **E-Commerce:** Machine learning can help to boost online sales with the help of recommendation systems (that recommend relevant products to potential customers), analytics and predictions (to learn from past sales and improve future sales), etc.

- **Autonomous cars:** Cars that drive themselves will no longer be a thing of the future. They already exist, and in a few years will be available on the market for anyone and everyone to access.

- **Manufacturing:** Many companies use robots to develop their products in a quicker and more convenient manner. This is because robots can be programmed to work tirelessly, with more accuracy, and at less cost.

- **Healthcare:** AI technology has improved immensely, and a major piece of evidence of that is the fact that it is now being implemented in healthcare. One very interesting application is robotic arm surgery, where, as the name suggests, a robotic arm is used to conduct surgery. Starting with the use of the Arthrobot in 1985, this type of surgery has been conducted several times to facilitate increased precision and decreased incision.

Summary

We now know what machine learning is and how it makes use of data with the help of data science techniques. We have gone through some types of machine learning algorithms and have seen how they are applied in the world so far. With the rate at which our technology is advancing, the need for machine learning is growing immensely. This calls for better and more advanced methods of machine learning. One such part of machine learning is a widely used technique known as deep learning. We'll cover that in the next chapter.

## CHAPTER 3

Introduction to Deep Learning

Machine learning for artificial intelligence sounds pretty interesting so far, doesn't it? When I first heard about it, I thought it was something out of a science fiction movie. It's so amazing how things used to be experienced only in *reel* life, and now they can be experienced in *real* life too!

Oh, yes, that pun was definitely intended.

Once machine learning took off in the world of technology, there was no stopping it. Every day, every minute, people began making new discoveries and developing newer models that worked better than the ones that came before. However, these machine learning models were still not good enough. They worked, don't get me wrong. They were quite effective as well. But they just weren't efficient enough.

That was until people succeeded in developing a technique under machine learning that would help a machine to figure things out for itself, and thus solve extremely intricate problems with great accuracy. In fact, this technique became so popular it is now quite well known as an individual area under artificial intelligence (even though it is not separate from machine learning). It was soon given the name "deep learning."

In this chapter, we will see how this method of machine learning came about and why it is needed. We will also dive into the process involved in deep learning; that is, the working of neural networks. This will give us an understanding of why libraries like TensorFlow are important within a programming language, especially in the context of deep learning.

Origins of Deep Learning

Deep learning is a branch of machine learning that uses artificial neural networks to help the machine to think about and respond to a particular problem.

The important thing to remember here is that, although it is very tempting to think of deep learning as an independent area under artificial intelligence, it is definitely not. It is very much a part of artificial intelligence, and is a subset of machine learning (Figure 3-1).

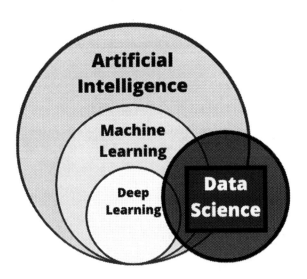

Figure 3-1. *Deep learning is a subset of machine learning within the artificial intelligence sphere*

Thus, we can say that deep learning is a subset of machine learning, which is a subset of artificial intelligence. Data science is like a common denominator here, as it is a necessary part of all three areas. The origins of deep learning can be credited to Walter Pitts and Warren McCulloch.

Walter Pitts was a logician in computational neuroscience, while Warren McCulloch was a neurophysiologist and cybernetician.

In the year 1943, they created a computer model that was inspired by the neural networks present in the human brain. They developed something called threshold logic, which was a combination of mathematics and algorithms that compared the total input with a certain threshold. This enabled them to recreate the process of thinking, just as it happens in the brain. This was a breakthrough that led to many more deep learning innovations.

Let us now learn about a very important aspect of it known as neural networks.

Neural Networks

The neural network, or artificial neural network, was inspired by and modeled after the biological neural network. These networks, like the human brain, learn to perform specific tasks without being explicitly programmed.

A neural network is composed of a series of neurons that are connected together to form a type of network, hence the name neural network. A neuron, or an artificial neuron, is the fundamental unit of a neural network. It is a mathematical function that replicates the neurons in the human brain, as you can see in Figure 3-2. Table 3-1 provides a comparison of biological and artificial neurons.

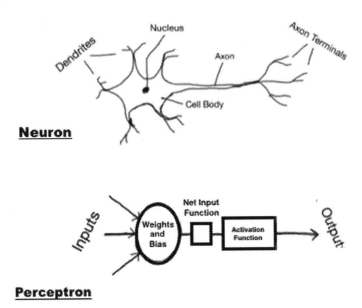

Figure 3-2. *A biological neuron and an artificial neuron*

Note   A perceptron is nothing but an artificial neuron. In deep learning, the terms *perceptron* and *neuron* are used interchangeably.

Table 3-1. *Comparison of a Biological Neuron and an Artificial Neuron*

Biological Neuron	Artificial Neuron
It receives information in the form of electrical signals.	It receives information in the form of numerical values.
Literally speaking, the brain consists of about 86 billion biological neurons.	A neural network can consist of a maximum of about 1,000 artificial neurons.
The general composition is a cell body, dendrites, and axon.	The general composition is the weights and bias, the net input function, and the activation function.

Working of an Artificial Neuron (Perceptron)

The perceptron follows a particular flow of steps in order to achieve its desired output. Let's go through these steps one by one to understand how a perceptron works.

Step 1: Accepting Inputs

The perceptron accepts inputs from the user in the form of digital signals provided to it. These inputs are the "features" that will be used for training the model. They are represented by $x(n)$, where n is the number of the feature. These inputs are then fed to the first layer of the neural network through a process called forward propagation.

Step 2: Setting the Weights and Bias

Weights: The weights are calculated and set while training the model. They are represented by $w(n)$, where n is the number of the weight. For example, the first weight will be $w1$, the second weight will be $w2$, and so on.

Bias: The bias is used to train a model with higher speed and accuracy. We generally represent it with $w0$.

Step 3: Calculating the Net Input Function

The equation for the net input function is as follows:

$$I = Sum(x(n).w(n) + w0)$$

Thus, each input feature is multiplied by its corresponding weight, and the sum of all these products is taken. Then, the bias is added to this result.

The Perceptron Learning Rule: According to this rule, the algorithm automatically determines the optimum values for the weights. The input features are then multiplied by these weights in order to determine if the perceptron should forward the signal or not. The perceptron is fed with several signals, and if the resultant sum of these signals exceeds a particular threshold, it either returns an output signal or doesn't.

Step 4: Passing the Values Through the Activation Function

The activation function helps with providing nonlinearity to the perceptron. There are three types of activation functions that can be used: ReLU, Sigmoid, and Softmax.

ReLU

The Rectified Linear Unit is used to eliminate negative values from our outputs.

If the output is positive, it will leave it as it is.

If the output is negative, it will display a zero.

Pros:

1. It is scalable.

2. It provides efficient computation.

3. It works well for neural networks with complex datasets.

Cons:

1. The output value is not restricted, which means it can cause issues if large values are passed through it.

2. The neurons can become inactive and "die" when the learning rate is large.

3. There is asymmetric handling of data, and results can end up inconsistent.

Sigmoid

It is a special mathematical function that produces an output with a probability of either 1 or 0.

Pros:

1. It is differentiable and monotonic.

2. It can be used for binary classification.

3. It is useful when we need to find only the probability.

Cons:

1. It does not give precise values.

2. There is the issue of a vanishing gradient, which prevents the sigmoid function from being used in multi-layered networks.

3. The model can get stuck in a local minima during its training.

Softmax

It is generally used in the final layer of a neural network. It is generally used to convert the outputs to values that, when summed up, result in 1. Thus, these values will lie between 0 and 1.

Pros:

1. It can be used for multi-class classification.

2. The range is only between 0 and 1, thus simplifying our work.

Cons:

1. It does not support a null class.

2. It does not work for linearly separable data.

One Hot Encoding

One Hot Encoding is a tweak that can be used while producing the outputs. It is used to round off the highest value to 1, while making the other values 0. This makes it easier to figure out which is the necessary class, as it is easier to spot a 1 from a list of 0s, rather than finding the highest value from a random list of numbers.

For example, say we have a set of inputs like 0.11, 0.71, 0.03, 0.15. Here, it is obviously not too difficult to identify the highest value since there are only four values.

Now imagine if the list had about 1,000 values. That would be difficult, wouldn't it?

But, with the help of One Hot Encoding, we can easily identify the one from the zeroes. That is why it is a popular technique used in neural networks.

> **Pro Tip**   The most common practice is to use a ReLU activation function in all the hidden layers, and then to use either a Softmax activation function (for multi-class classification) or Sigmoid activation function (for binary classification).

Step 5: Producing the Output

The final output is then passed from the last hidden layer to the output layer, which is then displayed to the user.

Now that we know how a perceptron works, let's go a little more in depth as to how a neural network performs a deep learning task.

Digging Deeper into Neural Networks

Deep learning goes a step further in machine learning. It allows the machine to begin thinking on its own in order to make decisions and carry out certain tasks. Neural networks are used to develop and train deep learning models. For example, consider a very simple neural network, which consists of an input layer, an output layer, and one layer of neurons, known as the hidden layer (as shown in Figure 3-3). The basic function of these three sections is as follows:

1. The **input layer**, as the name implies, is made of the input signals that will be further transmitted into the neural network.

2. The **hidden layer** is where all the important computations occur. The input that is fed to it is taken, calculations are performed on it, and then this input is sent to the next layer, which is the

output layer. The hidden layer can have any number
of neurons within it. There can also be more than
one hidden layer, depending on our requirements
and arrangement.

3. The **output layer**, as the name suggests, contains
the output signals. These are nothing but the final
results of all the calculations performed by the
hidden layer/s.

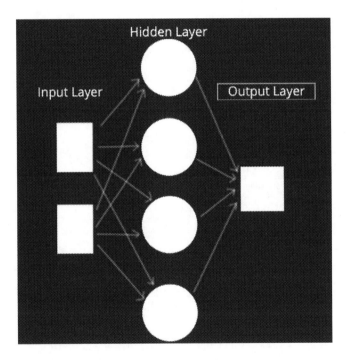

Figure 3-3. *Basic neural network*

The Process

There are four main steps to the neural network process that allow it to
come up with the most optimal solution for any problem that is given to it.

Step 1: The numerical input signals are passed into the neural network's hidden layers.

Step 2: The net input function is calculated with the weights and the bias that are generated during the training.

Step 3: The activation function is applied to the net input function.

Step 4: The result is then produced as the output of the neural network.

Thus, deep learning, as a part of machine learning, stands out as an extremely useful technique in the area of artificial intelligence.

Additional Concepts

In the following sections, we will review some key concepts that are important to know when it comes to neural networks.

Gradient Descent

Gradient descent is a deep learning algorithm that is used for optimization. It determines the values of the parameters of a function in order to ensure that the value of the cost function is minimized.

It minimizes the function by iteratively moving in such a way that it follows the path of steepest descent, depending on the negative of the gradient.

The gradient of the error function with respect to the weights of the neural network is calculated. Afterward, the output is compared with the labels in order to calculate the error.

Forward Propagation

A perceptron accepts inputs or "features," processes them, and then predicts the output. This output is then compared with the labels to measure the error. This is known as the forward propagation.

The data is fed into a layer of the neural network, passed through the activation function, and then fed to the next layer. The data must move forward to ensure that an output is achieved.

Thus, for any hidden layer in a neural network, after the first layer, the input is nothing but the output that is generated from the previous layer.

Back Propagation

Back propagation of the error is a deep learning algorithm that is used in training a supervised learning model. It calculates the gradient of the loss function corresponding to the weights generated by the network for a single input and output pair. It modifies the values of the weights in order to minimize the loss. It is an efficient method of calculation, and thus makes it feasible to use gradient methods to train multi-layer networks.

The algorithm computes the gradient of the loss function with respect to each weight by the chain rule, by proceeding one layer at a time. It iterates backward from the final layer. This is done to avoid redundant calculations during the process.

Overfitting

Overfitting is a statistical concept. It occurs when an analysis is said to be too accurate with respect to the data provided to it, and thus it can result in an improperly trained model. When we train our model, we may get very high accuracy. However, when testing the model, we may find a drastic difference in the accuracy. This is the result of overfitting.

It can happen when we train a model too many times, or with too little data. The model ends up getting very familiar with the training data and can thus achieve a very high accuracy with it. However, it messes up anyway when it comes to making predictions on new data, because it has still not been trained in the right way.

Types of Neural Networks

There are several types of neural networks, all based on their structure, composition, and flow. Let's go ahead and discuss a few of the common and most important ones that are used by deep learning developers.

Single-Layer Neural Networks: A Perceptron

The perceptron is the oldest single-layer neural network. As you have seen before, it takes the input from the user, multiplies it by the corresponding weight, adds that to the bias to get the net input function, and then passes the result through the activation function to get the final output. Every perceptron produces only a single output.

This type of neural network is not very efficient due to its extremely limited complexity. Thus, researchers came up with a model that contained more than one layer of perceptrons.

Multi-Layer Neural Networks

This type of neural network is used mainly for natural language processing, speech recognition, image recognition, etc. It consists of two or more layers of perceptrons, as follows:

- **Input layer:** This is all the available numerical data that is fed into the system and then transferred to the rest of the neural network.

- **Hidden layers:** This is where all the neurons are located. Every layer can have any amount of neurons. They are known as "hidden" layers because they remain hidden within the neural network as they perform the necessary computations.

- **Output layer:** This is the final result of all the calculations that happened in the hidden layers.

Convolutional Neural Networks

Convolutional neural networks follow the same principle as multi-layer neural networks, the only difference being that they include "convolutional layers," which make use of filters.

A filter is a grid of size AxB that is moved across the image and gets multiplied several times by it to produce a new value. Each value represents a line or an edge in the image.

Once the filters have been used on the image, its important characteristics can be extracted. This is done with the help of a pooling layer. These layers pool or collect the main features of each image. One popular technique of doing this is known as max pooling, which takes the largest number of each image and stores it in a separate grid. It thus compresses the main features into a single image and then passes it on to a regular multi-layer neural network for further processing.

These neural networks are mainly used for image classification. They can also be used in search engines and recommender systems.

Recurrent Neural Networks

Recurrent neural networks (RNNs) are used for temporal data; i.e., data that requires past experiences to predict future outcomes. State matrices remember previous states of data by storing the last output, and then use this data to calculate the new output.

Long short-term memory (LSTM) networks save the state matrices in two states: long term and short term. RNNs begin in the layers after the first layer. Here, each node acts as a memory cell during the computation, which allows it to compare previous values with new values during back propagation. These neural networks can be used for stock market predictions, natural language processing, and price determination.

Sequence-to-Sequence Models

A sequence-to-sequence model is mainly used when the lengths of the input data and output data are unequal.

It makes use of two recurrent neural networks, along with an encoder and a decoder. The encoder processes the input data, while the decoder processes the output data.

These models are usually used for chatbots and machine translation.

Modular Neural Networks

Modular neural networks have several different networks that each work independently to complete a part of the entire task. These networks are not connected to each other, and so do not interact with each other during this process.

This helps in reducing the amount of time taken to perform the computation by distributing the work done by each network. Each sub-task would require only a portion of the total time, power, and resources needed to complete the work.

Task Time   Have a look at the other types of neural networks. How do they differ from one another? How would a machine learning developer choose between these models?

Summary

Deep learning is a vast topic, and it is not possible to cover everything in detail within a single chapter. It suffices, however, to at least learn the basics of it, which is what we have done.

We learned what a deep learning neural network is and how it works. In addition, we discussed a few extra concepts that are important to know with regard to the functioning of neural networks. Finally, we went through several types of neural networks, which gave us a clearer understanding of how they can be developed and used for various purposes. Despite the fact that deep learning is a part of machine learning, these two terms are often used as if they are completely different entities. This can be quite confusing, especially for beginners. Thus, in the next chapter, we will see how they can be compared to one another.

CHAPTER 4

Machine Learning vs. Deep Learning

In the previous chapters, we learned that artificial intelligence involves the phenomenon of thinking machines. Machine learning is the technique of helping a machine to think so it is able to perform actions on its own. We also learned that deep learning is a type of machine learning that uses neural networks to help a machine learn. These neural networks are modeled after the human brain.

That said, you now may be wondering: Why would we compare machine learning and deep learning when they are not independent, but rather the latter is a subset of the former?

Well, as you've seen, traditional machine learning has several methods. Deep learning is one such method that is much more advanced in the way it works, and thus the procedure and results may vary. In this short chapter, we will discuss the differences between traditional machine learning and deep learning, which will help us understand when to use each method, as per our requirements.

© Nikita Silaparasetty 2020
N. Silaparasetty, *Machine Learning Concepts with Python
and the Jupyter Notebook Environment*, https://doi.org/10.1007/978-1-4842-5967-2_4

Factors Used When Comparing Machine Learning and Deep Learning

First of all, we need to understand that there are six characteristics based on which we will be comparing machine learning and deep learning. Of course, these aren't necessarily the only factors, as there are several other factors that differentiate one from the other. However, for the sake of getting a clear idea of how the two differ from each other, we will take into consideration these six aspects. Let's go through them briefly and see what they are.

- **Quantity of data required:** This refers to the amount of data that is needed for the process of learning. In some cases, we may have massive amounts of data that we have collected from various sources, and that we desire to use for our analysis. In other cases, we may have slightly less data with which we will need to perform our analysis.

- **Accuracy:** The main objective of every machine learning and deep learning problem is to obtain the highest accuracy, while ensuring that the model has not reached a state of overfitting. That said, our results can vary depending on the method, algorithm, technique, and data that we use. One method may give us higher accuracy, while another method may not.

- **Computational power:** The machines that are being trained require plenty of computational power in order to effectively perform their task. Earlier, when machine learning had just been invented, machines were slower and had less capacity. This resulted in inefficient outcomes. Nowadays, however, machines have improved. It is thus possible to carry out our computations with tremendous computational power.

- **Cognitive ability:** This refers to the ability of the machine to understand its inaccuracies and sort out the issue on its own. If a machine does not have this ability, it will not be able to make corrections to its parameters and/or structure, and a programmer will have to step in and do it for the machine.

- **Hardware requirements:** This refers to the type of hardware equipment needed by the algorithms to carry out their respective operations. This mainly depends on how advanced the program is, and on what the outcome is expected to be.

- **Time taken:** This refers to the amount of time taken, first to train the model, and then to validate it. This can vary according to the different parameters and algorithms used. By modifying them, we can either increase or decrease the amount of time taken to train and test the model.

Now that we are aware of the various factors that we will be considering to compare our models and what exactly each factor refers to, we can move on to exploring the differences between machine learning and deep learning.

Differentiating Between Regular Machine Learning and Deep Learning

Before we begin, we must remember that these are not necessarily the only factors involved in differentiating between machine learning and deep learning, especially considering that the entire process is a highly advanced area of technology, which means that there are many intricacies involved. However, we will keep our comparison simple but informative, so as to easily comprehend the differences between the two processes. Thus, taking into consideration the six factors mentioned earlier, we will now see how machine learning and deep learning vary from each other.

Quantity of Data Required

In general, machine learning requires plenty of data for the machine to successfully train itself. However, in traditional machine learning, we do not need to have too much data. We just need enough to enable the machine to process, learn, and act. On the other hand, deep learning needs larger amounts of data. This is to ensure that the machine has enough information to develop inferences on its own, without any external aid. See Figure 4-1.

Less Data Required   **More Data Required**

Figure 4-1. *Comparison of data requirements*

Accuracy

Accuracy, as you likely already understand, is the measure of how correct or precise the machine is when coming up with a solution. Although both methods give results that are quite precise, as you can see in Figure 4-2, regular machine learning is relatively less accurate, since it uses a smaller amount of data from which to learn and make inferences. Deep learning is much more accurate due to the large amount of data that it uses to learn and make inferences.

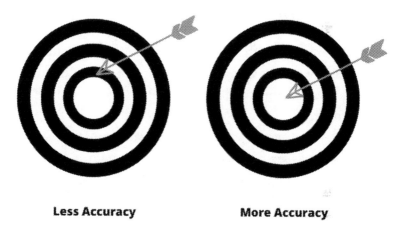

Less Accuracy   **More Accuracy**

Figure 4-2. *Comparison of accuracy*

Computational Power

Both machine learning and deep learning require a lot of computational power in order to train their models with the data given to them. However, the amount of power required by regular machine learning programs is comparatively less, mainly due to the fact that it uses less data for its computations. Deep learning requires more power to analyze its data and train its model. See Figure 4-3.

Less Computational Power   **More Computational Power**

Figure 4-3. *Comparison of computational power*

Cognitive Ability

One of the most important differences between machine learning and deep learning is that their cognitive abilities vary. Machine learning models have a lower cognitive ability because if they happen to make an inaccurate prediction, external assistance (in this case, a programmer) is required to make the necessary changes and then retrain the model. Deep learning models, however, have a higher cognitive ability because they can figure out inaccuracies and make the necessary changes on their own, without the need of a programmer. See Figure 4-4.

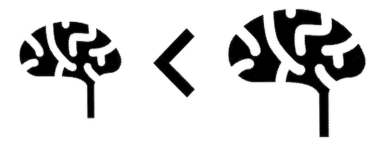

Lesser Cognitive Ability   **Greater Cognitive Ability**

Figure 4-4. *Comparison of cognitive ability*

Hardware Requirements

Most traditional machine learning algorithms can run smoothly on low-end systems. They do not depend too much on sophisticated machinery to carry out their processes. Deep learning algorithms, on the other hand, depend heavily on the hardware that is used because they need GPUs to optimize their processes. Therefore, they would need high-end machines for their operations. See Figure 4-5.

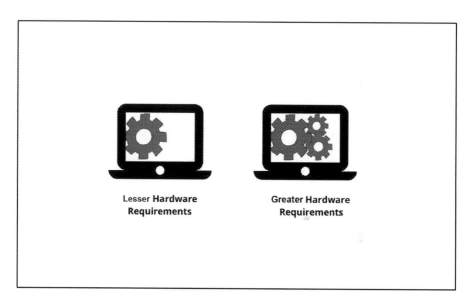

Lesser **Hardware**
Requirements

Greater **Hardware**
Requirements

Figure 4-5. *Comparison of hardware requirements*

Time Taken

Although this may not be true in all cases, it is a generally known fact that machine learning models take less time to train, while deep learning models take a longer time. This occurs mainly because deep learning models consist of more parameters, which means that the machine has a lot more work to do with regard to learning from its data. Machine learning models, however, don't have too many parameters, and so it is easier for the algorithm to compute.

When it comes to validation of the models, deep learning tends to be faster, whereas machine learning is slower. Once again, this differs from case to case. See Figure 4-6.

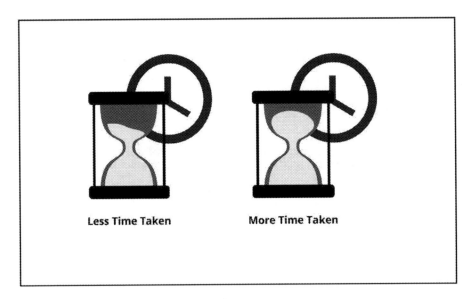

Less Time Taken   **More Time Taken**

Figure 4-6. *Comparison of time taken*

Summary

We have seen six ways in which deep learning differs from machine learning. It is now easy to understand why many people consider both areas to be extremely important in the field of artificial intelligence. Depending on the kind of input and technology available, people can choose the type of machine learning method they want to employ.

We can now move on to the process involved in setting up the system to help it learn. This is where the programming part comes in. Machine learning requires programmers to use data science techniques, followed by some specific machine learning algorithms, to enable the machine to think on its own. All this can be done within one single program.

We can use several programming languages to carry out our machine learning tasks, like Python, Java, C++, Julia, and R. However, since Python has emerged as one of the most popular machine learning programming languages so far, we shall be having a look at it over the next few chapters in the context of machine learning and deep learning.

CHAPTER 5

Machine Learning With Python

In previous chapters, we saw what artificial intelligence is and how machine learning and deep learning techniques are used to train machines to become smart. In these next few chapters, we will learn how machines are trained to take data, process it, analyze it, and develop inferences from it.

Machines need to be programmed to carry out particular actions. There are about 700 major and minor programming languages in the world to date. These languages have developed over the years according to the needs of the time. Many of the languages are just new and improved versions of older languages. As computers and computer-related businesses grew, the need for programming languages increased as well.

As artificial intelligence evolved, the usefulness of a programming language for machine training became an added criteria for its popularity. As of 2019, the top three languages were Java, Python, and C/C++. Excluding C, the other languages are object oriented.

Note Object-oriented programming (OOP) is a type of programming in which data is stored in objects as fields or attributes, and code is stored as methods or procedures.

OOP is a common method of programming because it is scalable, reusable, and efficient.

© Nikita Silaparasetty 2020
N. Silaparasetty, *Machine Learning Concepts with Python and the Jupyter Notebook Environment*, https://doi.org/10.1007/978-1-4842-5967-2_5

In this book, we will be learning how to program machines with the help of Python, which is, at present, one of the most widely used languages when it comes to machine learning. We will start by getting acquainted with this programming language.

Introduction to Python

Python was first developed and released in the year 1990 by Guido van Rossum, a Dutch mathematician, at the Centrum Wiskunde & Informatica in the Netherlands. One very interesting fact to note is that the name Python was, surprisingly, not taken from the notorious reptile, but rather from the equally notorious comedy group Monty Python that Guido was fond of.

According to the official Python website, "Python is an interpreted, object-oriented, high-level programming language with dynamic semantics."

In simpler terms,

- it is an interpreted language, which means it allows instructions to be executed freely and directly, without any prior compilation required;

- it uses objects that contain data and code;

- it follows a language style that is easy for human beings to interpret; and

- it allows information to be updated according to time.

Python's popularity first peaked around 2003, and ever since then it has retained its position as a highly acclaimed programming language. Its popularity can mainly be attributed to its features, which are listed in the next section.

Key Python Features

Python was mainly developed to improve code readability and to reduce the amount of coding required to program a machine. Apart from this, it has a variety of unique features and provisions that make our overall programming experience smooth and easy.

These features include the following:

- **Open source license:** This means it is free to download, modify, and redistribute under an OSI-approved license.

- **Readability:** It has a very easy-to-read syntax.

- **Cross-platform working:** It can run on any operating system, including Linux, Windows, Mac OS, etc.

- **Extensive standard library:** It consists of many useful libraries that can be used for a variety of applications.

- **Easily integrated:** It can easily be integrated with other languages like C, C++, Java, etc.

- **Supports object-oriented and procedure-oriented programming:** It primarily follows OOP, but it also makes room for POP, which is one of the most unique features of Python.

- **Allows GUI programming:** It has several libraries that allow users to develop graphic user interfaces quickly and easily.

- **Large community:** It has a huge community of coders, making it easier to make improvements, get help, solve issues, and develop new ideas.

Fun Fact   The community of Python users who support the language, and, more specifically, those who are experts in coding with help of Python, are known as Pythonistas.

Python's Competitors

As mentioned earlier, there are multitudes of other programming languages that are used in various fields and for various purposes. In the area of machine learning for artificial intelligence, some common programming languages that people use, other than Python, include the following:

- **R:** It is mainly used for visual representations, as graphs can be created very easily with just a few lines of code. It thus allows for exploratory data analysis.

- **Java:** It is one of the oldest languages in the world of computer programming. It is great in terms of speed, reliability, and security.

- **Scala:** Its runtime is extremely fast, and it can be used to develop complex pieces of code. It is moderately easy for a beginner to pick up.

- **Julia:** It is high level, scalable, dynamic, and quick. It also provides some powerful native tools that can be implemented for machine learning.

- **C++:** It has a high speed, a sufficient set of libraries and tools, and is most efficient when it comes to using statistical techniques.

Python as a Preferred Language for Machine Learning

Machine learning can become quite a complex process, especially when the data is massive, the model is extensive, and the objective is challenging. That said, it requires a language that simplifies its process and makes it less tedious for the developer.

When compared to other programming languages, Python stands out for the following reasons:

- It works seamlessly across different platforms. Thus, developers need not worry about using only one platform. They can easily distribute and use the Python code. A lot of other languages don't offer this feature, or are limited in their cross-platform abilities, and hence need to be used only on a single platform.

- It consists of a vast list of machine learning–specific libraries, utilities, and frameworks, which can be used by developers to make their programming faster and easier. Other languages don't have such an extensive selection.

- Its code is simple, readable, and concise. It is, therefore, easier for a developer to focus their attention on the machine learning problem at hand, rather than having to worry too much about writing the correct code and following the correct syntax, which most of the other languages require.

- It has a large community of developers who frequently use the language. This makes it less of a task for us to ask questions about any issues that arise while programming. It also allows Python developers to come together to discuss tips and ideas with one another. Other programming languages either have a smaller community or no community at all.

Python's Machine Learning Libraries

First, we will understand what a library is.

A library in the programming world is a collection of methods and functions that allow a user to perform various tasks without having to write the necessary code for it.

We use libraries to save time while we program. Python has a huge array of open source machine learning libraries, including, but not limited to, the following:

- **Pandas:** The Pandas library provides users with the ability to handle large datasets. It provides tools for reading and writing data, cleaning and altering data, and so on.

- **Numpy:** The Numpy, or Numerical Python, library provides users with a powerful array of computing abilities. It tackles the problem of slow mathematical computations and allows users to perform huge calculations with the help of multi-dimensional arrays.

- **Scipy:** The Scipy library is used for scientific and technical computations. It works on Numpy's multi-dimensional arrays.

- **Scikit-Learn:** The Scikit-Learn library consists of various features and methods that have specially been made to assist users in their machine learning requirements. It makes use of the Numpy library, specifically when it comes to array operations.

- **TensorFlow:** The TensorFlow library is an increasingly popular library that provides users with a large set of flexible and accessible tools for machine learning. You will be learning more about TensorFlow later on in this book.

With the help of these libraries, we can develop our machine learning program quickly and easily.

Other Applications of Python

Due to the diverse functionality of Python as a programming language, its utility is not limited to artificial intelligence alone. It is used for a variety of other applications as well. Some of these applications include the following:

- Web development

- Data analysis

- Educational purposes

- Software testing

- Computer graphics

- Game development

- Scientific and numeric computing

- Desktop GUIs

Installing Python

As mentioned before, Python is free to download. There are several ways to download and install Python onto your system, based on your OS and your preference.

One method of installing Python is from the official Python website, which provides an installer that users can download and run on their computers.

Another method of installing Python is with the help of package installers like Homebrew that make installation more convenient.

In this book, we will learn a very easy way to do it—with the help of an application known as Anaconda.

Anaconda is an open source distribution of the Python and R programming languages. It is free for us to download and use on our system.

It was created to make our machine learning process easier, mainly by making package installation simpler. It has an easy-to-use interface and comes with Python pre-installed on it. It also makes our task of installing the Jupyter Notebook application much easier, as we will see in the next chapter.

Let us now learn how Anaconda can be installed onto our systems.

Installing Python with Anaconda

Before we begin, we must have a look at the system requirements given in the Anaconda documentation, just to make sure that our system will be able to support Anaconda without any trouble. To download Anaconda, we need to follow these steps:

1. Go to the Anaconda website (`https://www.`
    `anaconda.com/distribution/`) and find the
    download option for your OS, as shown in Figure 5-1.

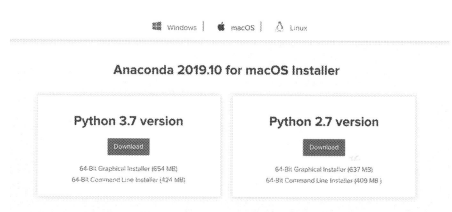

Figure 5-1. *Choosing the right version to download and install*

2. Since Anaconda comes pre-installed with Python, it
    gives you the option to select the version of Python
    that you want to install when you download the
    Anaconda application. Select the latest Python
    version available and click on the Download button.
    Here, I have selected Python 3.7 for my Mac OS.

3. Once Anaconda is downloaded, locate the file on
    the computer and double-click on it to begin the
    installation.

4. Once the installation is completed, you will be able
    to see the Anaconda Navigator icon in your list of
    applications. Click on it.

5. You will see a screen showing you a couple of useful programming-related applications. You will also see that, by default, a base (root) environment has been created that contains Python and its libraries.

6. It is always good to create a new working environment, other than the base. To do so, click on the Create button. In the dialog box that appears, you can give your new environment a name, select your Python version, and then click the Create button, as shown in Figure 5-2.

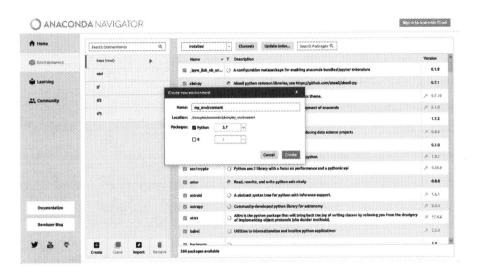

Figure 5-2. *Creating a new Python environment*

7. Once your environment is created, you need to select it as your working environment. Once you do that, you will be able to see a list of installed and uninstalled packages by clicking on "Environments," then choosing the "Installed" or "Not installed" option accordingly from the drop-down menu at the

top, as shown in Figure 5-3 and Figure 5-4. You can even search for a specific package by entering its name.

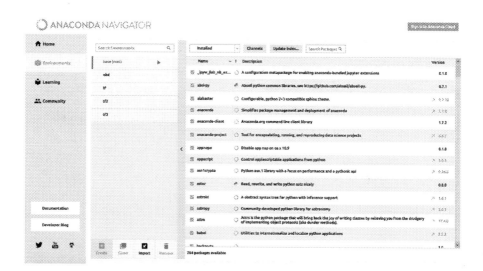

Figure 5-3. *List of installed packages*

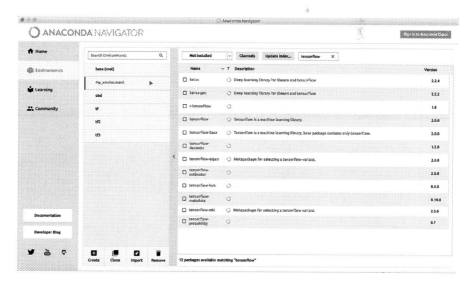

Figure 5-4. *List of uninstalled packages*

8. You can now begin installing some of the necessary libraries that you will need for machine learning, including Pandas, NumPy, SciPy, Scikit-learn, TensorFlow, Matplotlib, and Seaborn. Search for these libraries, select them by clicking on the check box to their left, then click the Apply button, as shown in Figure 5-5.

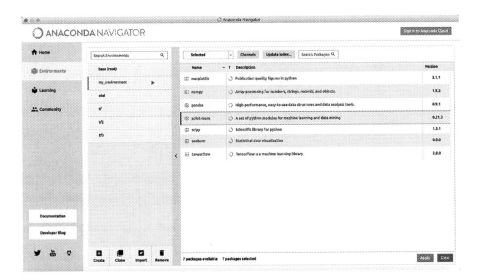

Figure 5-5. *List of selected packages to be installed*

There you have it! Your Python environment is now downloaded, installed, and ready for use!

Python Interpreters

One of the key features of Python is that it is an interpreted language, while other programming languages like Java, C, and C++ are all compiled languages.

Let's understand the difference between the two.

A compiled language takes the entire program and translates it from machine code to source code in order to obtain the required output. These languages therefore have a faster runtime, but are not cross-platform.

An interpreted language executes the code directly by reading each line one by one and then running it to obtain the required output. These languages therefore have a slightly slower runtime, but are cross-platform.

There are newer technologies being developed to tackle this issue of slow runtime, like the "just-in-time" compiler, which compiles the program during its execution instead of before it.

Now, when we say that Python is an interpreted language, it does not mean that it is not compiled at all. Compilation happens for a Python program, but it is not explicitly shown to the programmer. The code is compiled into bytecode, which is a low-level form of the original code. This bytecode is then executed by the Python virtual machine.

In this way, Python runs the code directly, is not restricted to a particular platform, and is not too slow with regard to execution speed.

There are several types of interpreters that Python can use to run a program. Let's have a brief look some of the most common ones:

1. **CPython:** This is the default implementation of Python. It is most popularly used as it is most compatible with Python packages and with extension modules that are written in C. It is the reference implementation of Python, which means that all the different versions of Python are implemented in C.

2. **Jython** (formerly JPython)**:** This is an implementation of Python that is written in Java and Python. It translates Python code into Java bytecode, and then executes it on a Java virtual machine. This allows Python code to run on Java platforms. It also allows users to use a Java class like a Python module.

3. **IronPython:** This is an implementation of Python that was developed for Microsoft's .NET framework. It uses Python libraries as well as .NET framework libraries. It also provides an interactive console and dynamic compilation support for improved performance.

4. **PyPy:** This Python implementation was written in RPython, which is a subset of the Python programming language. It uses a just-in-time compiler, which gives it a quick runtime speed. It is meant to provide maximum compatibility with CPython, while strengthening performance.

5. **Stackless Python:** This implementation was, like CPython, written with Python and C. It gets its name from the fact that it does not depend on the C call for its stack. It uses the C stack between function calls, and then clears it out. It makes use of microthreads, and supports task serialization, tasklets, communication channels, and more.

6. **MicroPython:** This is a small, open source Python implementation that was written in C and is compatible with Python 3. It allows us to write simple Python code instead of complex low-level language code, and it can be run on microcontroller hardware. It has a range of modules from Python's standard library, as well as some extra libraries that are specific to MicroPython, which can be used to program the board.

Now that we know what interpreters are, we need to know how to interact with them. One of the most generic ways to do so is by using something known as a Python shell.

The Python Shell

In computing, a shell acts as a medium between the user and the interpreter. With the help of the shell, the programmer can input some code and receive the necessary output. The shell waits for the user to enter a command or a line of code. It then executes this code and displays the obtained result.

It is called a shell because it is the outermost layer of the operating system. It can provide users with either a command-line interface (CLI) or a graphical user interface (GUI), depending on what is required for that particular operation.

The Python shell, or the Python interactive shell, also called the Python REPL shell, takes a Python command and executes it, displaying the required outcome. The term *REPL* is an acronym for the systematic flow of events that occurs during this process, as follows:

- **Read:** It reads or takes in an input from the user.

- **Eval:** It evaluates the input.

- **Print:** It prints or displays the output to the user.

- **Loop:** It loops or repeats the process.

This shell interface is meant to be simple, easy, and great for beginners to get the hang of programming on a computer.

Opening the Python Shell

This task is much easier than it sounds. It is basically a two-step process that can be accomplished in a flash.

1. First, you need to open the command-line interface of your operating system. For example, on Mac OS and Linux, it would be the Terminal, while on Windows, it would be the command prompt. See Figure 5-6.

81

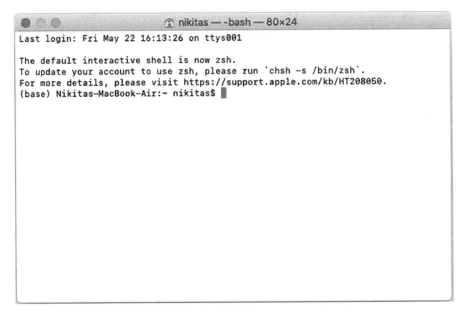

Figure 5-6. The Mac OS Terminal

2. Next, in this interface, type the following:

python

Hit the Enter key. This should give the output shown in Figure 5-7.

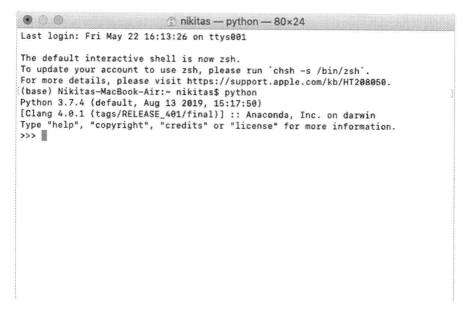

Figure 5-7. *The Python shell*

We are now in the Python REPL shell! This is one of the simplest interfaces that we can use to program with Python. This Python shell can now accept input as a Python command and execute it to display the necessary output. Some simple examples are shown in Figure 5-8, where I have performed some single-digit arithmetic operations (addition and subtraction).

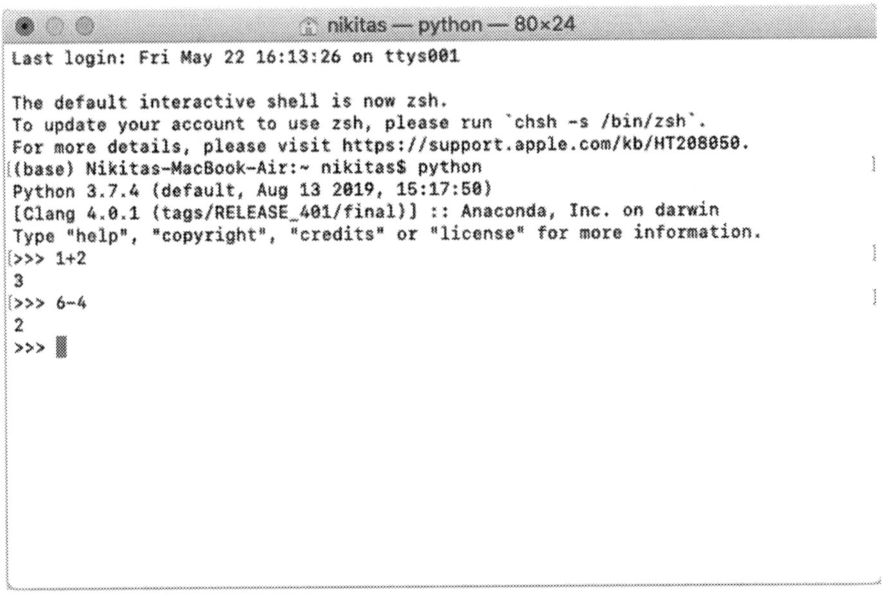

Figure 5-8. *Arithmetic operations in the Python shell*

We can use the help() command to explore different features within Python. To exit the Help window and return to the Python shell, press q and then Enter. See Figure 5-9.

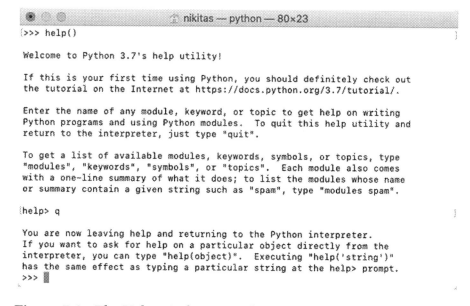

```
● ○ ○                    🏠 nikitas — python — 80×23
>>> help()

Welcome to Python 3.7's help utility!

If this is your first time using Python, you should definitely check out
the tutorial on the Internet at https://docs.python.org/3.7/tutorial/.

Enter the name of any module, keyword, or topic to get help on writing
Python programs and using Python modules.  To quit this help utility and
return to the interpreter, just type "quit".

To get a list of available modules, keywords, symbols, or topics, type
"modules", "keywords", "symbols", or "topics".  Each module also comes
with a one-line summary of what it does; to list the modules whose name
or summary contain a given string such as "spam", type "modules spam".

help> q

You are now leaving help and returning to the Python interpreter.
If you want to ask for help on a particular object directly from the
interpreter, you can type "help(object)".  Executing "help('string')"
has the same effect as typing a particular string at the help> prompt.
>>> █
```

Figure 5-9. *The Help window in Python*

Exiting the Python Shell

Once we are done programming with Python, we will need to exit the Python programming environment by closing the shell. We can do this by typing in the following command:

`exit()`

This exits the Python interactive shell and returns back to the main command-line interface of the OS. The reason we use the brackets at the end of the command is because we are calling the exit function in order to exit from the shell. See Figure 5-10.

```
● ● ○                    🏠 nikitas — -bash — 80×24
Last login: Fri May 22 16:13:26 on ttys001

The default interactive shell is now zsh.
To update your account to use zsh, please run `chsh -s /bin/zsh`.
For more details, please visit https://support.apple.com/kb/HT208050.
(base) Nikitas-MacBook-Air:~ nikitas$ python
Python 3.7.4 (default, Aug 13 2019, 15:17:50)
[Clang 4.0.1 (tags/RELEASE_401/final)] :: Anaconda, Inc. on darwin
Type "help", "copyright", "credits" or "license" for more information.
>>> 1+2
3
>>> 6-4
2
>>> exit()
(base) Nikitas-MacBook-Air:~ nikitas$ █
```

Figure 5-10. *Exiting the Python shell*

The keyboard shortcut for this step is `ctrl+D` on Mac OS and Linux, and `ctrl+Z+Enter` on Windows.

Summary

In this chapter, we covered the fundamentals of Python as a programming language. We read about its origins, its characteristics, its importance in the machine learning world, and its competitors. We skimmed through some of its machine learning libraries, as well as its other non-ML applications, just to get a better idea of what it can do. We then learned how to install it onto our systems and set it up. We also had a look at some common Python interpreters that are used for programming, and we had a peek at the Python REPL shell.

We must realize, however, that in order to use Python effectively for machine learning programming, the Python shell will not be of much use, since it is mainly meant for short commands and simple coding.

We will thus need to set up a lucrative working environment in which we can enter and execute our Python code. Some popular applications that we can use for this are the Jupyter Notebook, PyCharm, Spyder, and IDLE. In this book, we will be using Jupyter Notebook for all our programming purposes.

Jupyter Notebook has begun to gain more and more popularity due to its simplicity, ease of use, and accessibility. It makes large-scale programming and code distribution so much easier and quicker. It is also very easy to install, especially with the help of Anaconda.

That said, let's take a look at what Jupyter Notebook is and how it makes our coding experience better, especially when it comes to Python programming for data science and machine learning.

Quick Links

Learn more about Python: `https://www.python.org/about/`

Python vs. Other Programming Languages: `https://www.python.org/doc/essays/comparisons/`

Python Documentation: `https://www.python.org/doc/`

Python Events: `https://www.python.org/events/python-events`

Learn more about Anaconda: `anaconda.com/why-anaconda/`

PART II

The Jupyter Notebook

In Part II, we will get ourselves acquainted with the Jupyter Notebook application. We will go through its setup, take a look at its features, and get hands-on experience in using this interface for Python programming.

What to expect from this part:

- An introduction to the Jupyter Notebook application

- How to install and set up Jupyter Notebook

- Explore the features of Jupyter Notebook

- Learn how to use Jupyter Notebook

- Use Python programs with the help of Jupyter Notebook

CHAPTER 6

Introduction to Jupyter Notebook

In the previous chapter, we learned about Python. We also had a glance at how we can use Python in its REPL shell to write our code. This Python shell, however, is not the most recommended tool to use when it comes to massive machine learning programming. This is why we have developed applications like Jupyter Notebook, which aid in such programming requirements.

Jupyter Notebook is the brainchild of Project Jupyter, which is a non-profit organization founded by Fernando Pérez. It was created with the objective of developing open source software and providing services that allow multiple languages to interact with one another for effective computing.

Jupyter Notebook is an open source web-based application that allows users to create, edit, run, and share their code with ease. This application gets its name from the main languages that it supports: Julia, Python, and R.

To fully appreciate Jupyter Notebook, let us first take a look at what a "notebook" is with regard to programming.

© Nikita Silaparasetty 2020
N. Silaparasetty, *Machine Learning Concepts with Python
and the Jupyter Notebook Environment*, https://doi.org/10.1007/978-1-4842-5967-2_6

Understanding the Notebook Interface

A computational notebook or a notebook interface, or quite simply a notebook, is used for literate programming, where we add a comprehensive explanation along with our program. It is a virtual notebook; i.e., it has a notebook-style GUI that provides a word processing software's functionality, along with a kernel and a shell.

A Brief History of the Notebook

The notebook interface was first introduced around 1988, when Wolfram Mathematica 1.0 was released on the Macintosh. This system allowed users to create and edit notebook interfaces through its front-end GUI.

Then came Maple, released for Macintosh with version 4.3. It provided a GUI in the style of a notebook, which became a highly acclaimed interface for programming.

As the notebook began to grow in demand, people soon began to adapt notebook-styled kernels and backends for other programming languages, such as Python, MATLAB, SQL, and so on. Thus, the computational notebook became quite popular among coders.

Features of a Notebook

The generic features of a notebook are as follows:

1. It allows us to add cells of code, which make debugging and programming easier.

2. It can be used to display visual representations of data.

3. It allows us to add text in between each cell, which makes it easier for the coder to explain the function of each line of code.

4. Items within a notebook can easily be rearranged for narrative purposes and better readability.

5. It can be used as a tool for live presentations.

6. It can be used to create interactive reports on collected data and analytical results.

Commonly Used Notebooks

Some commonly used open-source notebooks include the following:

1. Jupyter Notebook

2. IPython

3. Apache Spark Notebook

4. Apache Zeppelin

5. JupyterLab

6. R Markdown

An Overview of Jupyter Notebook

As mentioned before, Jupyter Notebook is a web-based application developed by Project Jupyter. Its aim is to enable users to, as stated on the official website, *"create and share documents that contain live code, equations, visualizations and narrative text."*

Jupyter Notebook was developed in 2014 as a spin-off of the original IPython, which is a command shell used to carry out interactive coding. With the release of Jupyter Notebook, IPython found itself competing with it, to an extent. It still remained as a kernel for Jupyter and as a shell for Python, but everything else came under Jupyter Notebook.

Fun Fact   Jupyter Notebook was originally known as IPython Notebook, since it was conceived from IPython.

The official website of Project Jupyter states that Jupyter Notebook can support over forty programming languages. Each project is stored as a notebook consisting of several cells of code, graphs, texts, and equations, which can be altered easily. These notebooks can also be conveniently distributed to others.

Features of Jupyter Notebook

Apart from the generic characteristics of a computational notebook, Jupyter Notebook has the following key features:

1. Each Jupyter Notebook is a JSON document. JSON is a language-independent data format that is derived from JavaScript. It uses human-readable text to transmit data containing arrays or attribute–value pairs.

2. Each Jupyter Notebook is usually saved with a `.ipynb` extension.

3. Jupyter Notebook is similar in style to other interfaces that originated years before it, including Maple and Mathematica (from the 1980s) and SageMath (from the 2000s).

4. Jupyter Notebook was released under the modified BSD license, which provides users with minimum limitations in the usage and distribution of the software.

5. Jupyter Notebooks can easily be shared with others through email, Dropbox, GitHub, and the Jupyter Notebook Viewer.

6. Jupyter Notebook is, at present, completely free to use, and it is intended to remain free for anyone to use at any time.

Advantages of Jupyter Notebook

Jupyter Notebook has, since its release, proved to be a powerful tool for programming, especially for high-level programmers. It has a smooth and easy-to-use interface, which is great for those who are new to programming. It also allows users to create new files and folders directly on their system for easy storage of their code.

Let's take a better look at what makes Jupyter Notebook stand out as a programming application. It has the following features:

- It makes the overall programming experience better.

- It is an interactive application.

- It is open source; i.e., it is free to download, install, and use.

- It allows users to add notes, comments, and headings in between lines of code in a notebook in the markdown format, which is especially useful when sharing code with others.

- It is convenient to edit code as each line of code can be added to a separate cell, and this cell can be deleted, modified, replaced, and so on.

- It is very easy to share and distribute code with others.

- Each notebook can be converted into different file formats, like HTML, markdown, PDF, and so on.

Jupyter Notebook is in great demand now, but it did arrive pretty late into the programming world. Before its conception, there were other applications such as text editors and IDEs that coders used, and that are still in use even today.

Text Editors and IDEs

Earlier, programmers would type all of their code into a text editor like Windows Notepad. These text editors allowed them to type in their code and then install extra plugins that added bonus features. After that, they had to transfer all the code to the command prompt to run it.

Later, IDEs were created to give programmers an environment that provided them with all the features they would need to develop their code. They would not need to write and run their code in separate applications, or install new plugins each time. They could easily create, edit, debug, and run their code in a single workspace.

Let us first take a look at the classic text editors to see how they were used to program.

Getting Acquainted with Text Editors

Over the years, programmers have used all kinds of tools and environments for their code, including the very basic text editor.

The text editor is a computer program that is used, as its name suggests, to edit plain text.

They are usually provided by default with operating systems. They allow users to edit files like documentations and source code. Some examples of text editors are the TextEdit application on Mac OS, Vim on Linux, and the widely known Notepad on Windows.

Text editors are great for developers who are new to the field and who are still familiarizing themselves with coding. They are also readily available on the system. This is why most people prefer to start out with text editors.

However, with the increasing complexity of advanced programs, and especially with the introduction of artificial intelligence and machine learning, programmers felt the need to create workspaces that would make the process much easier. Hence, they came up with something called an IDE.

Getting Acquainted with the IDE

An IDE, or integrated development environment, allows us to write, edit, test, and debug our code by providing us with the necessary tools and services.

For example, with the help of an IDE, we can manage resources, debug errors, and complete our code very easily. Most IDEs are limited to a single programming language, but some allow users to work with multiple languages.

Features of an IDE

Most IDEs come with the following features:

1. **Text editor:** It allows users to write and edit code, and also provides syntax highlighting according to the language being used.

2. **Auto-completion of code:** It identifies the next possible input provided by the coder, and inserts that component accordingly. This reduces the chance of errors, and also significantly decreases the amount of time spent programming.

3. **Debugging tools:** They seek out any errors in the code and proceed to rectify them, thus saving time and making the programmer's work easier.

4. **Compilers:** They are used to translate the code into a format that the machine can understand and process.

Benefits of an IDE

Programming with an IDE is considered advantageous for the following reasons:

1. It is a single environment in which the programmer can access all the required tools and utilities.

2. It can auto-complete code and debug errors on its own, reducing the effort and time spent by the programmer.

3. It manages the syntax on its own as well, which is especially useful when it comes to indentations.

4. The code can be reverted, if needed, without any major inconvenience.

5. Project collaboration becomes easier.

Some Popular IDEs

Three of the most commonly used IDEs are the following:

- **IDLE:** IDLE, or the Integrated Development and Learning Environment, is automatically installed along with Python. It is lightweight and simple, making it easy to learn. It provides tools that are similar to those in text editors. It allows cross-platform usage and multi-window text editing. It is a good start for those who are new to IDEs.

- **Spyder:** Spyder, or the Scientific Python Development Environment, is an open source IDE. It is great for anyone who is a beginner to IDEs. It has the features of a text editor, but with a GUI, making it easy for people to transition from the simple programming application to this more advanced one. It even allows the installation of extra plugins for added benefit. It is also visually similar to RStudio, allowing people to switch easily from R to Python.

- **Pycharm:** Pycharm is a professional Python IDE. It was made by JetBrain. It provides code editors, error highlighting, and a debugger, all with a GUI. It can also be personalized by allowing the user to change its color, theme, and so on. It integrates Numpy and Matplotlib, making it easy to work with graphs and array viewers.

Note   Although IDEs have always been used to describe a working environment that allows a programmer to write and edit code, debug errors, and so on, the main definition of an IDE is slowly being altered as a result of the introduction of other tools such as Jupyter Notebook that also allow users to easily develop code.

IDE vs. Text Editor

Text editors have always been very simple to use. Even beginners to the programming world could easily use them to code, without having to worry about learning to use a new application. They required less effort in terms of understanding the programming interface.

IDEs, on the other hand, require a little bit of familiarization before a programmer can feel comfortable enough to make full use of its features. However, they have extra capabilities and tools that simplify the programming experience.

The conclusion: It all depends on our need and preference. If we don't want to spend time learning how to use an application, and would rather make use of a simple interface for our code, we can use a text editor. And, if we want to invest a little time in learning how to use an application, which will then help us later with the rest of our programming requirements, we can use an IDE.

Now that we know what text editors and IDEs are, we can see how the notebook interface, and specifically Jupyter Notebook, is more beneficial to programmers compared to similar applications.

Jupyter Notebook vs. Other Programming Applications

Why would we want to choose Jupyter Notebook over other programming applications? Well, let's have a look at the following differences between Jupyter Notebook and other such applications:

- **Tools:** Jupyter Notebook provides users with tools and utilities that make the programming experience much faster and easier. Compared to other IDEs, Jupyter Notebook has more services available.

- **Graphical User Interface:** The GUI of Jupyter Notebook varies because it is meant to look like a notebook and not like a general IDE. This makes it easier on the eye and quite simple to understand.

- **Usability:** It is easier to use Jupyter Notebook compared to other IDEs because of its easily accessible features.

- **Learning:** Compared to other IDEs, Jupyter Notebook may take a little time to grasp, just because of how different it is from what we are used to. However, once we do learn it, it becomes extremely convenient to use.

- **Web-based:** Jupyter Notebook runs on the browser, unlike other IDEs, which work on the local system.

- **Visualization:** Although some IDEs provide users with a great platform for visualization, other IDEs don't. Jupyter Notebook does, though, thus making it easier for a programmer to use plots and other such visualization techniques.

In this way, Jupyter Notebook outdoes its competitors in the programming world.

Jupyter Notebook sounds like a blast, doesn't it? Well, it is! Once we get the hang of it, we can thoroughly enjoy programming with it. Let's now learn how to set up our Jupyter Notebook environment on our machine.

Installing Jupyter Notebook

As mentioned in the previous chapter, one advantage of using Anaconda is that the installation of Jupyter Notebook becomes quite an easy task to achieve. There is no hassle of navigating through various applications just to download it. All we need to do is the following:

1. Open the Anaconda Navigator.

2. Select the working environment, as shown in Figure 6-1.

3.   Click on the option to install Jupyter Notebook.

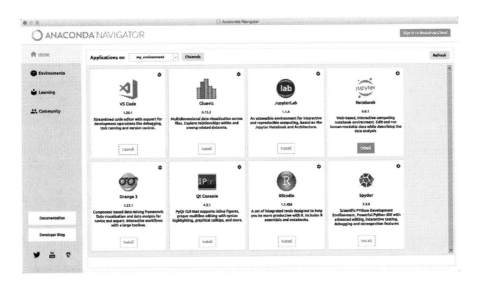

Figure 6-1. *Installing Jupyter Notebook*

Et voila! Jupyter Notebook is now ready for use. In the next few sections, we will explore its interface so as to get ourselves comfortable with the layout and working of the application.

Note   When installing, we must make sure that we install Jupyter Notebook and not JupyterLab. There's a difference!

Launching Jupyter Notebook

The first thing we will need to do is select our working environment. Here, I have chosen myenv.

Next, we need to open up the Jupyter Notebook window. We can do this by opening the Anaconda application and then clicking on "Launch" under the Jupyter Notebook icon.

Since Jupyter Notebook is a web-based application, it opens in our browser. The first window that opens is a dashboard, which gives us a glimpse of our work so far, including files, folders, and notebooks. It will look like Figure 6-2.

Figure 6-2. *The Jupyter Notebook Dashboard*

The URL bar contains a link that represents the notebook server, and indicates that it is running from our local machine. The link will appear like this this - `http://localhost:8888/tree`.

The rest of the dashboard is quite self-explanatory, but we will run through it anyway. Here's a breakdown of some of the basic but most important features of the Jupyter Notebook interface, as shown in Figure 6-3:

Figure 6-3. *Some important features of the Jupyter Notebook dashboard*

1. The Logout button allows us to log out of our Jupyter Notebook session.

2. The Upload button allows us to upload a readily available Jupyter Notebook that we can use.

3. The New button allows us to create a new Python notebook, file, folder, or terminal.

4. The File tab shows us an ordered list of all our files and folders.

5. The Running tab shows us any terminals or notebooks that are open and running.

6. The Name button allows us to toggle the way our list of files and folders is displayed; i.e., in ascending or descending alphabetical order.

7. We can even select the "Last Modified" option to display our items based on the last time that they were modified.

8. The little check-box option with a "0" beside it allows us to select all folders, notebooks, files, and items that are open and running. We can even select all of the items at once.

9. In our list of items, the ones with a folder icon next to them represent the folders that we have on our computer, as shown in Figure 6-4.

☐ ☐ Applications	18 days ago	
☐ ☐ Desktop	2 minutes ago	
☐ ☐ Documents	a day ago	
☐ ☐ Downloads	5 hours ago	
☐ ☐ Movies	18 days ago	
☐ ☐ Music	18 days ago	
☐ ☐ opt	18 days ago	
☐ ☐ Pictures	18 days ago	
☐ ☐ Public	18 days ago	

Figure 6-4. *List of folders*

10. Once we create Jupyter notebooks and text files,
they will begin to appear on the dashboard. The
items with a page icon next to them represent the
documents that have a .txt extension, and the ones
with a notebook icon next to them represent the
Jupyter notebooks, which have a .ipynb extension,
as shown in Figure 6-5.

☐ ▣ Very First Notebook.ipynb	seconds ago	555 B
☐ ☐ Very First Text File	seconds ago	0 B

Figure 6-5. *A notebook and a file*

Now that we are aware of the general features of the Jupyter Notebook
interface, let's see what happens when we select an item from our list by
clicking on the check box next to it. When we select an item, we will have a
number of available options, as shown in Figure 6-6:

Figure 6-6. *Controls available for each item*

105

1. We can Rename the item.

2. We can Duplicate the item to make another copy of it.

3. We can Move the item to another location.

4. We can Download the item.

5. We can View the item, which will open in a new tab in our browser window.

6. We can Edit the item.

7. We can Delete the item by clicking on the red trash can symbol.

8. We can Shutdown a notebook that is open and running, as shown in Figure 6-7.

Figure 6-7.   Option to shut a notebook down

9. We can even select several items at the same time and perform any available action on them.

Let us now create a brand new Jupyter notebook and explore all the features within it.

Inside a Jupyter Notebook

To create a new Jupyter Notebook, all we have to do is click on 'New' on the dashboard, and then select the kernel of our choice. Here, we select the 'Python 3' kernel, as shown in Figure 6-8.

Figure 6-8. *Opening a new Jupyter Notebook with a Python 3 Kernel*

We will get a new tab with a notebook user interface (UI) that looks like Figure 6-9.

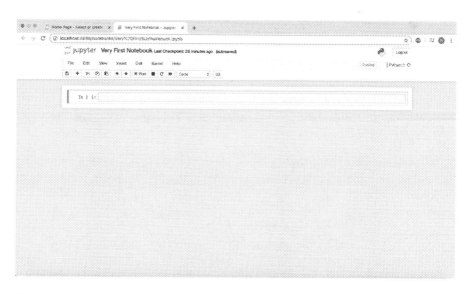

Figure 6-9. *A new notebook*

107

The notebook UI is quite self-explanatory as well. However, just like before, we will have a quick run-through of all its main features.

1. At the top, the title of the notebook is displayed. It starts out as "Untitled," and when we click on it, we can change the name based on our preference, as shown in Figure 6-10.

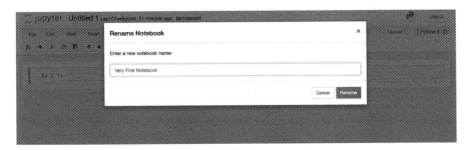

Figure 6-10. *Renaming a notebook*

2. Next to the title of our notebook, we will see "Last Checkpoint," with a timing. That indicates the last time the notebook was auto-saved.

3. Below this is the menu bar, containing a series of drop-down menus, as shown in Figure 6-11.

Figure 6-11. *The Menu Bar*

4. After this comes the tool bar, containing tools that we will need as we use Jupyter Notebook, as shown in Figure 6-12. We can hover over each tool icon to know what it does.

Figure 6-12. *The Tool Bar*

> 5. Finally, we have the area where we type in all of our input and view our output, as shown in Figure 6-13.

Figure 6-13. *This is where the different kinds of cells appear, allowing us to enter our input*

You might have noticed that the menu bar contains the Cell menu and the Kernel menu. These are two terms that are very important in the Jupyter Notebook environment.

Cell

A cell is nothing but the box in which we type all our input, which can either be code, regular text, or headings.

When we first open our Jupyter notebook, we will see that the first cell is a "Code" cell. This cell allows us to enter the commands, functions, variables, constants, and all other inputs that are a part of our program. When we execute this cell, the output, if any, is displayed beneath it.

Let's try typing the following in the "Code" cell:

```
print("Hello World!")
```

Now, we can execute the cell by clicking on the Run button from the tool bar. We can also just use the keyboard shortcut, which is Shift+Return. We will find that the code line is executed and the output is printed out right below the cell, as shown in Figure 6-14.

Figure 6-14. *Executing a code cell*

The second type of cell is a "Markdown" cell. Markdown is a formatting syntax that is used to style plain text. Thus, this cell is used to enter any text that is not a part of the code. This could be explanations or notes that are needed in between the code, either to make it easier for us as we program, or to make it more comprehensive for someone else who is going through it. Once we type in all the necessary text and execute the cell, it becomes a regular text box that is visible in our program.

Let's try this text in the "Markdown" cell:

Hello World!

Our Markdown cell will display an output as shown in Figure 6-15.

Figure 6-15. *Entering regular text*

The third type of cell is the "Heading" cell. This cell is used to add headings throughout our program. This allows us to make our entire program look much more organized, especially if we have more than one program running within the same notebook.

Let's try typing this in the "Heading" cell:

```
My Program
```

The heading will appear as shown in Figure 6-16.

Figure 6-16. *Entering a heading*

We can also just open a regular Markdown cell and type the following in -

```
# My Program
```

The '#' symbol is used to convert the sentence into a heading. The number of times we use the symbol indicates the level of the heading. For example, a single hash is used to obtain a level one heading.

We can change the type of cell that we want to use by selecting it from the list of options in the Tool Bar.

Kernel

A kernel runs the code that is contained within the Jupyter notebook.

A kernel is not limited to a single cell, but rather to the entire notebook. When we execute code in a selected cell, the code runs within the kernel and sends any output back to the cell to be displayed.

There are kernels for more than a hundred languages, including Python, C, R, and Java. When we create a new notebook from the Jupyter Notebook dashboard, we are basically selecting our kernel by choosing the Python version that we desire to use. In this case, when we select "Python 3," we are telling our system to open a Python 3 kernel.

Now that we have some idea of what a cell and a kernel are, let's come back to the menu bar and explore what the Cell and Kernel drop-down menus allow us to do.

The Cell Drop-Down Menu

Figure 6-17 shows the different options available within the Cell drop-down menu.

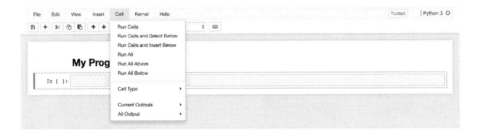

Figure 6-17. *Cell drop-down menu*

1. **Run Cells:** This executes the code that is in the selected cell or cells, and gives an output, if any.

2. **Run Cells and Select Below:** This executes the selected cells and then selects the cell below them.

3. **Run Cells and Insert Below:** This executes the selected cells and then inserts an extra cell just below them.

4. **Run All:** This executes all the cells in the notebook.

5. **Run All Above:** This runs all the cells that are above the selected cell.

6. **Run All Below:** This runs all the cells that are below the selected cell.

7. **Cell Type:** This allows us to select the type of cell you require.

8. **Current Outputs:** This gives us the option to either Toggle, Toggle Scrolling, or Clear the selected output.

9. **All Output:** This gives us the option to either Toggle, Toggle Scrolling, or Clear all the output in the notebook.

The Kernel Drop-Down Menu

Figure 6-18 shows the different options available within the Cell drop-down menu.

Figure 6-18. *Kernel drop-down menu*

1. **Interrupt:** This interrupts the running process as the code is being executed.

2. **Restart:** This restarts the entire kernel, retaining the previously obtained outputs.

3. **Restart and Clear Output:** This restarts the entire kernel, clearing the previously obtained outputs.

4. **Restart and Run All:** This restarts the entire kernel and once again proceeds to execute all the cells.

5. **Reconnect:** This allows the kernel to reconnect.

6. **Shutdown:** This shuts the active kernel down.

7. **Change Kernel:** This allows us to change our kernel to any version or language that we want.

There you have it! This was an overview of some of the most basic but important features of Jupyter Notebook.

Now that you are familiar with the working environment of Jupyter Notebook, let's go ahead and practice some Python programming with the help of Jupyter Notebook.

Additional Information

The Jupyter Project is a very interesting initiative, especially for data scientists and machine learning enthusiasts who need a reliable and convenient space to work on their projects. Let's have a look at two more very useful features that come under Project Jupyter, and that can be useful to some of us in our machine learning journey.

JupyterHub

JupyterHub allows multiple users to share resources in order to program. Each user has their own workspace where they can code without worrying about installations and maintenance.

It can run either on a user's system or on the cloud. It is customizable, flexible, portable, and scalable, making it a great interface for programmers. It also has its own community for users to discuss and contribute.

Jupyter nbviewer

Jupyter nbviewer is a free and publicly available instance of nbviewer, which is a web-based application that allows us to view a notebook as a static HTML web page. It also provides us with a link that we can use to share the notebook with others.

Apart from viewing a single notebook, we can also view notebook collections. These notebooks can even be converted into other formats.

Voila

Voila is used to convert a Jupyter notebook into a stand-alone web application that can be shared with others. It consists of an interactive dashboard that is customizable and allows users to view the notebook in a secure environment.

It can work in any Jupyter kernel, independent of the type of programming language used. It is a great choice for non-technical users who desire to view the results of the notebook without having to see the code cells or execute the code.

Google Colaboratory

Google's Colaboratory or Colab is a free online Jupyter environment. It runs in the cloud and stores its notebooks to the user's Google Drive.

As of October 2019, Colab mainly supports Python 2 and Python 3 kernels.

However, it is also possible for Colab to support R, Swift, and Julia.

Keyboard Shortcuts

First of all, you need to know that there are two modes of working with Jupyter Notebook, as follows:

- Command Mode, which allows us to navigate around the notebook with our arrow keys.

- Edit Mode, which allows us to edit the selected cell.

Table 6-1 lists some of the most useful keyboard shortcuts that we can use while working with Jupyter Notebook.

Table 6-1. *Keyboard Shortcuts for Jupyter Notebook*

Mac	Windows and Linux	Action
Cmd + Shift + P	Ctrl + Shift + P	Access keyboard shortcuts
Shift + Enter	Shift + Enter	Executes the code
Esc	Esc	Enters Command Mode when in Edit Mode
Enter	Enter	Enters Edit Mode when in Command Mode
A	A	Inserts a new cell above the selected cell while in Command Mode
B	B	Inserts a new cell below the selected cell while in Command Mode
D + D (Press D twice)	D + D (Press D twice)	Deletes the selected cell while in Command Mode
Shift + Tab	Shift + Tab	Displays the available documentation for the item entered into the cell
Ctrl + Shift + -	Ctrl + Shift + -	Splits the selected cell into two at the point where the cursor rests while in Edit Mode
F	F	Finds and replaces code while in Command Mode
Shift + J / Shift + Down	Shift + J / Shift + Down	Selects the chosen cell as well the cell below it
Shift + K / Shift + Up	Shift + K / Shift + Up	Selects the chosen cell as well as the one above it
Shift + M	Shift + M	Merges multiple cells

Summary

In this chapter, we have gained an understanding of the importance of the notebook interface, when compared to IDEs and text editors. We then explored the Jupyter Notebook application, its features, and its user interface.

The great thing about Jupyter Notebook is that it looks quite complex and technical, but in reality it is not too difficult to use, once you get the hang of it. Overall, it is a great tool to use for all your programming purposes. Not just that, it can also be used to display your results and present your output in a manner that is not too hard on the eyes.

In the next few chapters, we will begin some actual programming with the help of Jupyter Notebook. We will get a feel of how we can use the notebook interface effectively to enter, run, and debug our code. And, finally, once we have gained some familiarity with Jupyter Notebook, we will proceed with using the interface to develop our machine learning models.

Quick Links

Learn more about Project Jupyter: `https://jupyter.org/about`

Jupyter Documentation: `https://jupyter.org/documentation`

Try Jupyter: `https://jupyter.org/try`

JupyterHub: `https://jupyter.org/hub`

Jupyter Notebook Viewer: `https://nbviewer.jupyter.org/`

Google Colab: `https://colab.research.google.com/notebooks/intro.ipynb`

CHAPTER 7

Python Programming in Jupyter Notebook

In an earlier chapter, we learned all about the Python programming language. We studied its advantages, compared it with some other languages, and understood how its features make it stand out as a dependable language for machine learning.

In the previous chapter, we got acquainted with Jupyter Notebook, and we saw why it can be considered a suitable environment for building and executing programs that can train our machines. We also had a look at the layout of the Jupyter Notebook application.

In this chapter, we will get hands-on experience in combining Python with the Jupyter Notebook interface to effectively create, check, and run our machine learning models. Before we begin with the hardcore coding, however, we will start with some small-scale programs, just to refresh our generic programming knowledge and to understand the coding syntax of Python.

© Nikita Silaparasetty 2020
N. Silaparasetty, *Machine Learning Concepts with Python and the Jupyter Notebook Environment*, https://doi.org/10.1007/978-1-4842-5967-2_7

Opening a New Notebook

First things first, we need to open up a new Jupyter notebook with a Python 3 kernel, as shown in Figure 7-1.

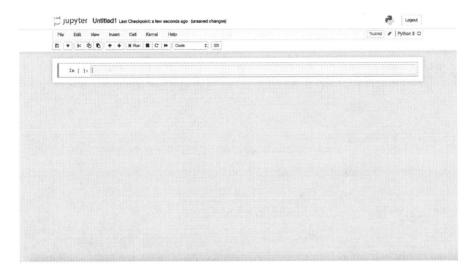

Figure 7-1. *A new Jupyter notebook*

Naming the Notebook

We can give our notebook a name, like "My First Jupyter Notebook" or "Python Programming with Jupyter Notebook" (Figure 7-2)

Figure 7-2. *Naming a new notebook*

Adding a Heading Cell

Now, let's give our first program a title. We will call it "Hello World." Do you remember how to convert a cell into a "Heading" cell?

That's right. We select the option from the tool bar. After that, we click on the cell and enter the title, as shown in Figure 7-3.

```
# Hello World
```

Figure 7-3. *Entering a program's title within a "Heading" cell*

The hash symbol (#) indicates that it is a level-one title.

Let's execute the cell. We can do this by clicking on the "Run" icon in the tool bar. A faster way of doing this is by using the keyboard shortcut Shift + Enter.

Now that our cell is executed, we will see the heading appear, as shown in Figure 7-4.

Hello World

```
In [ ]:
```

Figure 7-4. *Executing the "Heading" cell to add the title to the notebook*

Printing the Output of a Code Cell

The next cell automatically appears as a "Code" cell. Let's repeat the same code we used in the previous chapter by typing in the following:

```
print("Hello World")
```

Now when we execute the cell, we will get an output like this:

```
Hello World
```

Taking an Input from a User in a "Code" Cell

Let's see what happens when we take an input from a user. Type in the following code:

```
a = input("Enter your name: ")
```

Now when we execute the cell, we get the output shown in Figure 7-5.

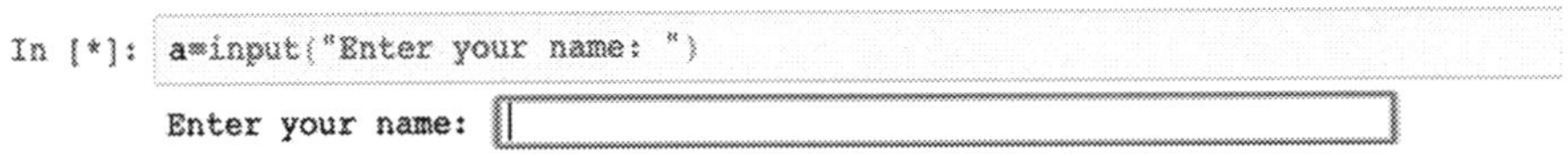

```
In [*]:  a=input("Enter your name: ")
         Enter your name: [                                  ]
```

Figure 7-5. *Waiting to accept an input from the user*

As you can see, the text that we have entered is displayed, followed by a text box where we can type in our input. This text box can accept any character that is typed in from the keyboard. The asterisk (*) at the left of the cell indicates that the program is still executing that cell. In this case, it is waiting for a command from the user before it can proceed. Once the user presses the Enter key, the program will continue executing.

After we finish typing and press the Enter key, the output will be displayed, as shown in Figure 7-6.

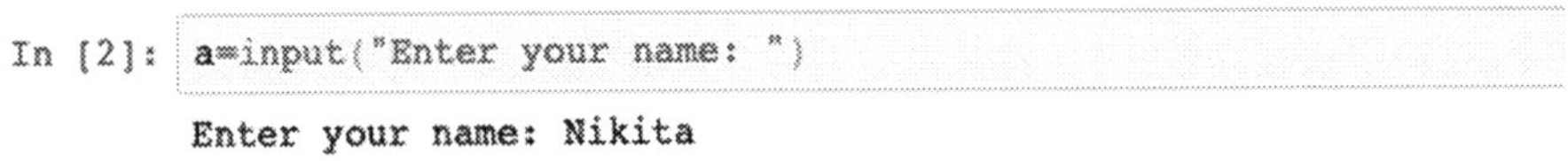

```
In [2]:  a=input("Enter your name: ")
         Enter your name: Nikita
```

Figure 7-6. *Displaying the accepted input*

Calling a Variable

When we accepted an input from the user, we stored it under the variable *a*. In the next cell, we will call this variable and display its output by typing the following:

```
a
```

Now when we execute the cell, we will get the value of *a* displayed, as shown in Figure 7-7.

```
In [3]: a
Out[3]: 'Nikita'
```

Figure 7-7. *Displaying the value of a variable*

Arithmetic Operations

Let's see what happens when we have some output to display, and also some input to take. We can explore this with the help of some simple arithmetic operations. Let's try the following code:

```
b=2

c=int(input("Enter a number: "))

sum=b+c

print(sum)
```

We will get a text box for the input, first, as shown in Figure 7-8.

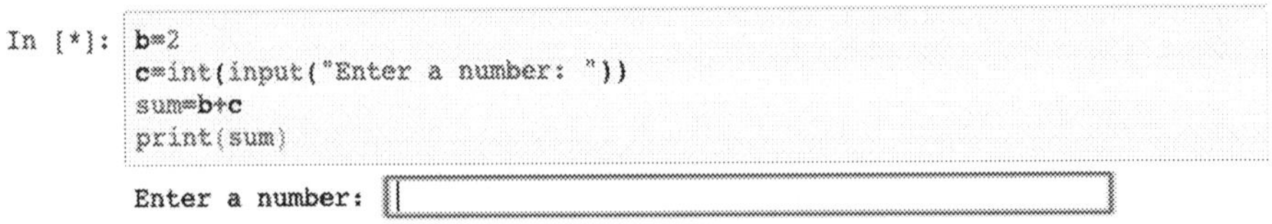

```
In [*]:  b=2
         c=int(input("Enter a number: "))
         sum=b+c
         print(sum)

         Enter a number: |
```

Figure 7-8. *Accepting a number from the user*

Once we provide the required value, the code performs the necessary calculation and displays the output, as shown in Figure 7-9.

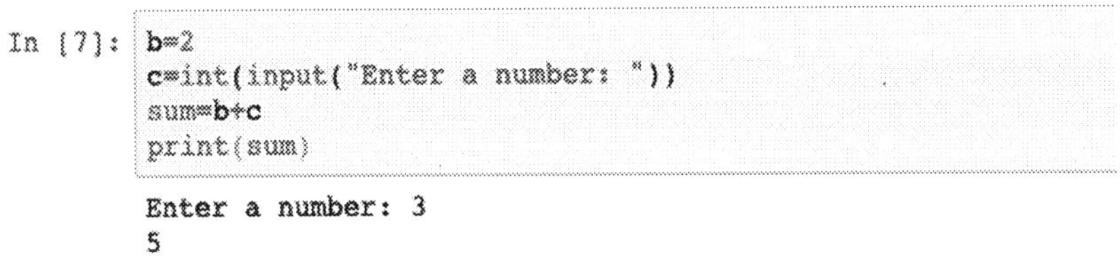

```
In [7]:  b=2
         c=int(input("Enter a number: "))
         sum=b+c
         print(sum)

         Enter a number: 3
         5
```

Figure 7-9. *Displaying the input as well as the result of the calculation*

We need to put int right before the input command to tell the program that we are expecting an integer from the user, which must then be used for the given arithmetic calculation. If we skip this step, there will be an error, because Python always inputs values as strings (including numbers and symbols), which prevents numbers from directly being used for the calculation.

Creating a Function

Now, let's create a function and see how that works. Type in the following code:

```
def prod(a):

    b=int(input("Enter a value: "))

    c=5

    p=a*b*c
    return(p)
```

When we execute this cell, we find that there is no output. There is, however, something happening behind the scenes. In the next cell, type this:

```
prod(6)
```

Remember, we can put any number that we want within the brackets. When we execute this cell, we will get a text box asking for a value. We can enter a value of our choice. When we press Enter, we will get the output shown in Figure 7-10.

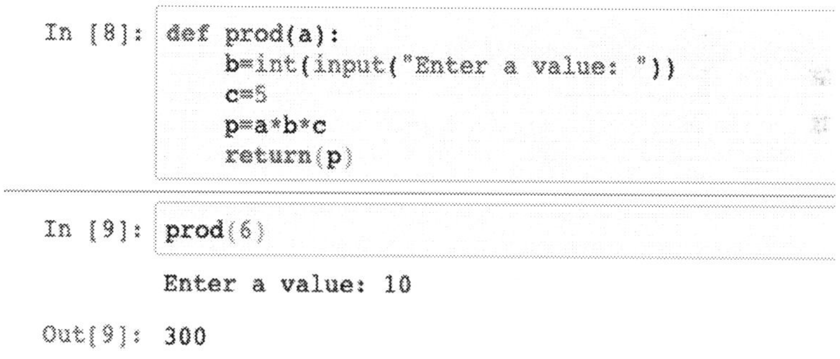

```
In [8]: def prod(a):
            b=int(input("Enter a value: "))
            c=5
            p=a*b*c
            return(p)

In [9]: prod(6)

        Enter a value: 10

Out[9]: 300
```

Figure 7-10. *Performing a calculation within a function, then calling the function to display the result*

Creating Lists

A list is an ordered set of items. We can create a list by entering all the required values between a pair of square brackets, as follows:

```
list = [2, 4, 6, 8, 10]

list
```

When we execute this, we will get an output as shown in Figure 7-11.

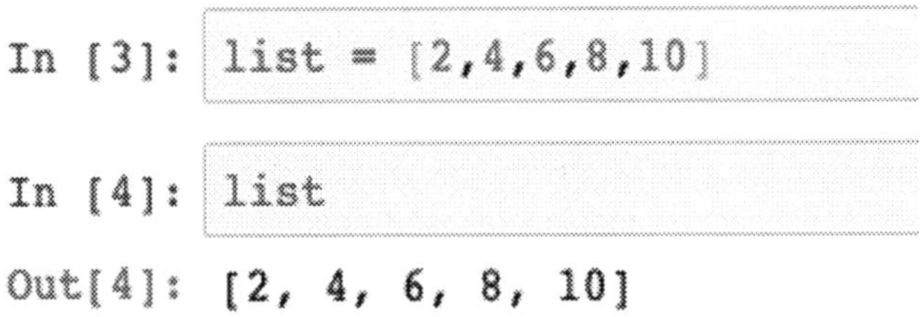

```
In [3]:  list = [2,4,6,8,10]

In [4]:  list
Out[4]:  [2, 4, 6, 8, 10]
```

Figure 7-11. *Creating a list*

Creating Dictionaries

A dictionary is an unordered set of items. We can create a dictionary by entering our values between a pair of curly brackets, as follows:

```
age = {"Henry":30, "Chiara":19, "Benedict":23, "Dominic":15,
"Gertrude":24}

age
```

When we execute this cell, we will get an output as shown in Figure 7-12.

```
In [33]:  age = {"Henry":30, "Chiara":19, "Benedict":23, "Dominic":15, "Gertrude":24}
          age

Out[33]:  {'Henry': 30, 'Chiara': 19, 'Benedict': 23, 'Dominic': 15, 'Gertrude': 24}
```

Figure 7-12. *Creating a dictionary*

Creating Loops

In programming, a loop is a set of instructions or steps that is continuously repeated until a condition is satisfied.

While Loop

Try typing in this code:

count=0

while count<=5:

    count=count+1

    print("Love your neighbour as yourself")

When we execute this cell, we will get an output as shown in Figure 7-13.

```
In [34]:  count=0
          while count<=5:
              count=count+1
              print("Love your neighbour as yourself")

          Love your neighbour as yourself
          Love your neighbour as yourself
          Love your neighbour as yourself
          Love your neighbour as yourself
          Love your neighbour as yourself
          Love your neighbour as yourself
```

Figure 7-13. *Running a while loop*

For Loop

Type this code into the code cell:

```
string=("Rejoice")

for i in string:

    print(i)
```

When we execute this cell, we will get an output as shown in Figure 7-14.

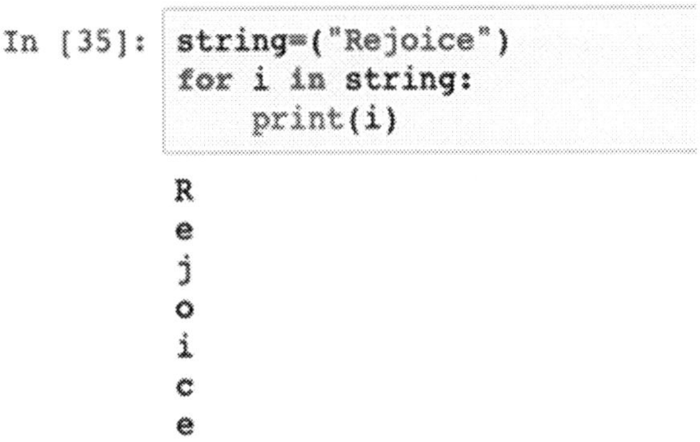

```
In [35]: string=("Rejoice")
         for i in string:
             print(i)

R
e
j
o
i
c
e
```

Figure 7-14. *Running a for loop*

Nested Loops

Nested loops consist of two or more loops used within a single code block.
    Enter the following code into the "Code" cell:

```
i=0

s=("Have a beautiful day")

while i<=3:

    i=i+1
```

```
for a in s:

    print(a)
```

When we execute this code, we will get an output as shown in Figure 7-15.

Figure 7-15. *Running nested loops*

Of course, for all practical purposes, I have not shown the full output. But it is easy to understand how the output will look, since the same sentence is printed out four times consecutively.

Adding Conditional Statements

In programming, a conditional statement is used to execute a particular step based on whether a specified condition is true or false.

If Statement

Type in this code:

```
x=3*2

if x%2 == 0:
    print("It is even")
```

When we run this code, we will get an output as shown in Figure 7-16.

```
In [37]:  x=3*2

          if x%2 == 0:
              print("It is even")

          It is even
```

Figure 7-16. *Executing an if condition*

The % symbol is used to find the remainder after division. So, on dividing by 2, if the remainder is 0, it indicates that the number is an even number.

Try changing the value of x to a number that is not divisible by 2, and see what happens.

If-Else Statement

We can use the same code as before, but with a minor addition to include the else condition, as follows:

```
x=3*3

if x%2== 0:
    print("It is even")
else:
    print("It is odd")
```

When we run this code, we will get an output as shown in Figure 7-17.

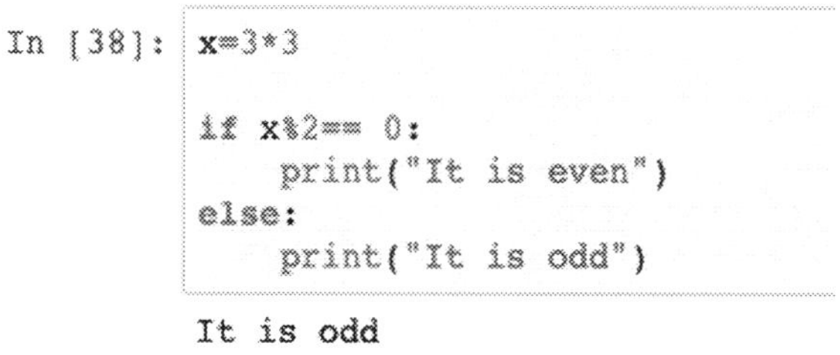

```
In [38]:  x=3*3

          if x%2== 0:
              print("It is even")
          else:
              print("It is odd")

It is odd
```

Figure 7-17. *Executing an if-else condition*

In this case, we add an extra condition, where we tell the program what to do if the first condition is not satisfied.

Elif Statement

This time we will use a slightly different code, as follows:

```
x=7

if x%2==0:

    print("It divisible by 2")
```

```
elif x%3==0:

    print("It is divisible by 3")

else:

    print("It is neither divisible by 2 nor 3")
```

When we run this program, we will get an output as shown in Figure 7-18.

```
In [39]:  x=7

          if x%2==0:
              print("It divisible by 2")
          elif x%3==0:
              print("It is divisible by 3")
          else:
              print("It is neither divisible by 2 nor 3")

          It is neither divisible by 2 nor 3
```

Figure 7-18. *Executing an elif condition*

Thus, `elif` allows us to supply our code with more than one condition. We can put `elif` several times throughout our code, depending on the number of conditions we have.

Adding Notes Within the Program

Sometimes, we may want to add some extra notes in between lines in our program, either for our own reference or to make sure that people who have access to it understand what they are going through. This is not the same as adding a regular "Markdown" cell. This is different because we are adding our notes within a "Code" cell. To do this, we need to add a hash (#) symbol before the code line. Here is an example:

```
# This is a comment line in between my code.
```

This line will appear in green italics in the "Code" cell, as shown in Figure 7-19.

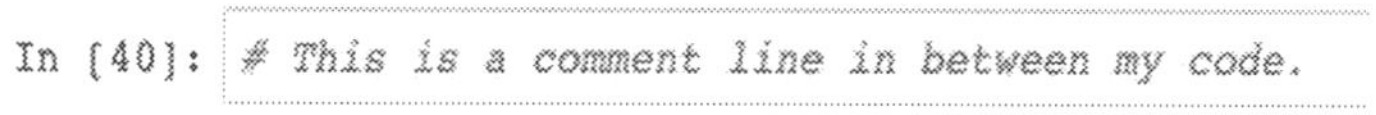

In [40]:   # This is a comment line in between my code.

Figure 7-19. *Adding a comment line within the code*

Deleting a Cell

Sometimes, we may have cells that are unnecessary. We can easily get rid of them by clicking on the scissor icon.

We can also do so by selecting the "Delete Cells" option from the "Edit" drop-down menu in the menu bar, as shown in Figure 7-20.

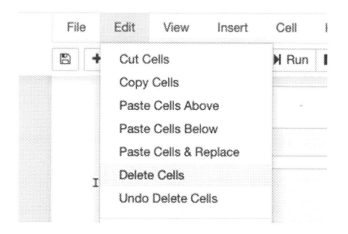

Figure 7-20. *Deleting cells using the drop-down menu option*

Adding a New Cell

We can even add a new cell beneath another cell by selecting that cell and then clicking on the "Insert Cell Below" icon or the plus sign.

The other way to do this is by selecting the "Insert Cell Below" option from the "Insert" drop-down menu in the menu bar. If we want to add a cell above the selected cell, we can either click on the "Insert Cell Below" icon followed by the "Move Cell Up" icon, or directly click on the "Insert Cell Above" option from the "Insert" drop-down menu, as shown in Figure 7-21.

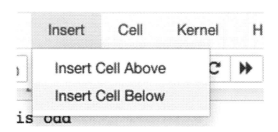

Figure 7-21. *Adding a new cell using the drop-down menu option*

Copying a Cell

We can also copy the contents of a cell and paste them in another cell with the help of the "Copy Selected Cells" and "Paste Selected Cells" options in the tool bar.

We can also do this by selecting the required options from the menu bar, as shown in Figure 7-22.

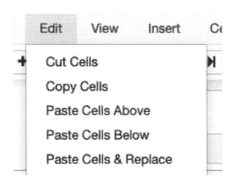

Figure 7-22. *Copying a cell using the drop-down menu option*

Moving a Cell

We may even want to switch the cells around, depending on our preference. We can shift cells up or down accordingly, using the up and down arrow icons in the tool bar.

We can also do this by going to the menu bar, clicking on "Edit," and then selecting either "Move Cell Up" or "Move Cell Down," as shown in Figure 7-23.

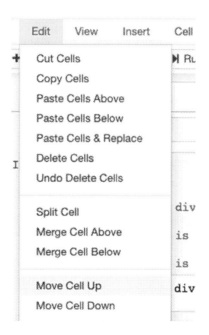

Figure 7-23. *Moving a cell using the drop-down menu option*

Merging Cells

Let us now go back to the previous few pieces of code, where we define a variable a as the input from a user, and then in the next "Code" cell print out the value of this variable.

Instead of carrying this out in two separate cells, we can just put this together in a single cell. The great thing is, we don't even have to retype or delete anything. All we need to do is go to the menu bar, select "Edit," then click on "Merge Cell Below," as shown in Figure 7-24.

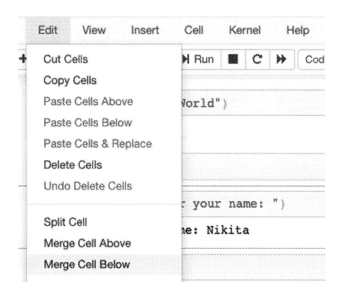

Figure 7-24. *Merging cells using the drop-down menu option*

Let's try this on one of our previous bits of code. Consider the code in which we take an input from a user, store it as input a, and then display the value of a. This was done in two separate cells of code. However, when we merge the cells, it puts the code together into a single cell, as shown in Figure 7-25.

```
In [2]:  a=input("Enter your name: ")

         a

         Enter your name: Nikita
```

Figure 7-25. *Two cells merged into a single cell*

Splitting a Cell

We can even split a cell into two parts using the "Split Cell" option from the "Edit" drop-down menu in the menu bar, as shown in Figure 7-26.

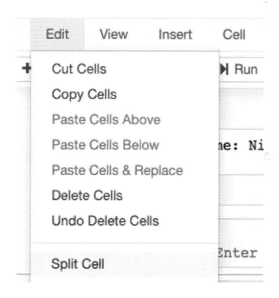

Figure 7-26. *Splitting a cell using the drop-down menu option*

First, click on the line from which point we want to split the code. Then click on the "Split Cell" option. The code will split, as shown in Figure 7-27.

```
In [ ]:   b=2
          c=int(input("Enter a number: "))
```

```
In [ ]:   sum=b+c
          print(sum)
```

Figure 7-27. *Splitting a cell using the drop-down menu option*

Running All Cells

Instead of executing each cell one by one, we can run them all at once. To do this, all we need to do is click on the "Run All" option from the "Cell" drop-down menu in the menu bar, as shown in Figure 7-28. This executes the entire notebook.

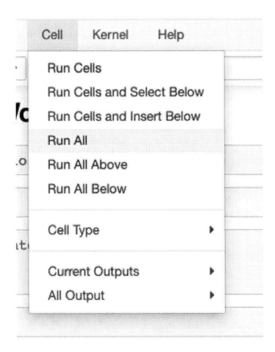

Figure 7-28. *Running all the cells in the notebook using the drop-down menu option*

Clearing the Current Output

To clear the output of the selected cell, click on the "Cell" option from the menu bar. Then, hover your cursor over "Current Outputs" in the drop-down menu, and in the sub-menu click on "Clear," as shown in Figure 7-29.

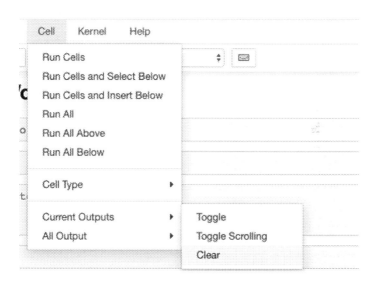

Figure 7-29. *Clearing the current output using the drop-down menu option*

Clearing All Outputs

To clear all the outputs in the notebook, click on the "Cell" option from the menu bar. Then, just like before, hover the cursor over the "All Output" option from the drop-down menu, and in the sub-menu click on "Clear," as shown in Figure 7-30.

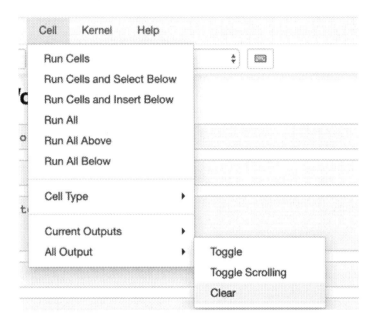

Figure 7-30. *Clearing all outputs using the drop-down menu option*

Restarting the Kernel

Sometimes, our program requires us to restart the kernel in order to get the desired output. It is similar to refreshing a page on our web browser. When we restart a kernel, we lose all the data stored in the variables.

To do this, first click on "Kernel" from the menu bar, then click on "Restart," as shown in Figure 7-31.

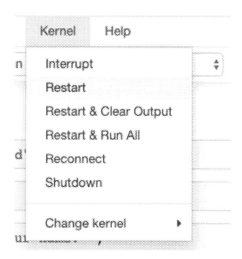

Figure 7-31. *Restarting the kernel using the drop-down menu option*

Here, we find that the kernel restarts, but the previous outputs of each cell execution are still displayed. If we don't want the outputs to remain, we will need to restart the kernel and also clear the outputs. We have the option of doing this in a single step, rather than in two steps.

Restarting the Kernel and Clearing the Output

To simultaneously restart the kernel and clear the output, click on "Kernel" from the menu bar, followed by "Restart & Clear Output," as shown in Figure 7-32.

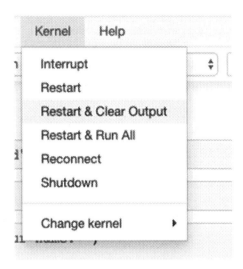

Figure 7-32. *Restarting the kernel and clearing the output using the drop-down menu option*

Interrupting the Kernel

I have found this feature to be extremely useful, mainly for machine learning. Sometimes, while our machine learning program is running, we may suddenly decide that we want to stop the process and start over. This could be due to an error that we suddenly find in the code, a decision to change certain variables, and so on. In such cases, all we need to do is interrupt the kernel by clicking on the "Kernel" option in the menu bar, followed by "Interrupt" in the drop-down menu, as shown in Figure 7-33.

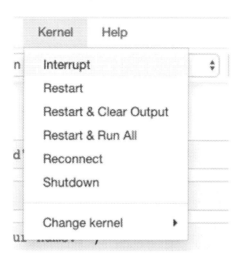

Figure 7-33. *Interrupting the kernel using the option from the drop-down menu*

The Help Menu

If we need any extra help regarding the general Jupyter Notebook UI, the keyboard shortcuts that we can use, and some of the machine learning libraries that are frequently used with Python, we can access the Help menu from the menu bar. A drop-down menu will open, as shown in Figure 7-34.

Figure 7-34. *Accessing the Help menu*

From this menu, we can select the option that we need help with. As you can see, the help options include topics related to the Jupyter Notebook application, as well as to Python libraries.

Summary

Well, there we go! We are now a lot more familiar with the user interface of Jupyter Notebook. We have also had a run-through of some important concepts related to programming, and we have seen how to code basic functions, like lists and loops, using Python.

With that under our belts, it's finally time to get the ball rolling as we step into Python's machine learning libraries. We have already read about how Python has a vast selection of libraries that can be called into a program. Moving ahead, we will be focusing our attention on one such library that has become increasingly sought after. Over the years, it has gained the approval of several developers due to its unique features, which make the process of machine learning much more effortless. This library is none other than TensorFlow, which, in the coming chapters, we will be using to program our deep learning models.

PART III

The TensorFlow Library

In Part III, we will dive into the TensorFlow library. Starting with an introduction to this widely used deep learning package, we will make our way towards its initial version that has been in use since its release. We will then get into TensorFlow 2.0, its distinguishing features, and a quick guide on how to migrate code from the previous version to the new version. The final chapter will lead us through a couple of deep learning programs with which we will use TensorFlow in Python and the Jupyter Notebook interface. This will help us to put it into practice all that we have learned throughout the book.

What to expect from this part:

- An introduction to the TensorFlow Library so far

- Program with the TensorFlow Library (version 1.0)

- An introduction to TensorFlow 2.0

- Migrating from TensorFlow 1.0 to TensorFlow 2.0

- Using TensorFlow to develop machine learning models (focusing on deep learning neural networks)

CHAPTER 8

The Tensorflow Machine Learning Library

To recap what was stated in an earlier chapter, Python has a huge variety of machine learning libraries that can be implemented in a program. These libraries serve various purposes—mathematical, scientific, graphical, and so on. Depending on the nature and the need of the program we are developing, we can call these libraries into our program.

We know that machine learning involves data science techniques (like cleaning, manipulating, and visualizing data), mathematical techniques, and statistical techniques. Keeping this in mind, some of the most commonly used Python libraries for machine learning include Matplotlib, Seaborn, Pandas, Scikit-learn, Numpy, Scipy, and so on.

These libraries have been tried and tested and were found to be easy to work with. They have thus gained popularity over the years, with numerous applications in various machine learning programs.

With the growing enthusiasm toward deep learning, there arose a need to create libraries that could assist with building multi-layered neural networks. Thus, libraries like Theano, Pytorch, Caffe, Keras, and TensorFlow were released. These libraries enable programmers to develop large, multi-layered neural networks with less time and effort, and more efficiency.

© Nikita Silaparasetty 2020
N. Silaparasetty, *Machine Learning Concepts with Python and the Jupyter Notebook Environment*, https://doi.org/10.1007/978-1-4842-5967-2_8

In this chapter, we will explore the TensorFlow library to get an overview of what it is, why it was developed, and how it has proved useful in the realm of artificial intelligence. We will then see how to install it on our system.

TensorFlow at a Glance

TensorFlow was developed by the Google Brain Team as a step up from the original DistBelief system, which was a closed-sourced software used for machine learning with deep neural networks. According to the official website:

> *"TensorFlow is an end-to-end open source platform for machine learning. It has a comprehensive, flexible ecosystem of tools, libraries and community resources that lets research-ers push the state-of-the-art in ML and developers easily build and deploy ML-powered applications."*

In other words, TensorFlow is an open source library that employs machine learning and deep learning techniques for large-scale computations. It involves the use of "tensors," which help in making our calculations simpler. We will delve deeper into that in the next section.

Fun Fact   TensorFlow was not, in actuality, meant for public access. It was only meant to be used by the Google Brain Team for their own research. It was, however, finally released to the public on November 9, 2015.

TensorFlow was released under Apache License 2.0. This means that people can use, modify, and distribute the software, as well as its modified versions, without worrying about royalties. All it requires for redistributions is an attribution notice. This is why the Apache License 2.0 is known as a copyleft license. It has minimum conditions for software redistribution and allows the software to be accessed, modified, and distributed, all for a common good.

TensorFlow consists of two main components, as follows:

1. *Tensors*, in which the data is held

2. *Flow*, referring to the computational graph

Let's see how the two work together to create large-scale deep learning models.

Tensors

Tensors can be defined as multi-dimensional arrays.

We might remember learning about dimensions in school. A dimension is roughly defined as the minimum number of coordinates that are needed to describe a particular point. In simpler words, it is the measure of the amount of space that an object occupies. For example, a line has only one dimension (length), while a square has two dimensions (length and width). In mathematics, we can have a number or a set of numbers arranged in various dimensions.

In mathematics and physics, we have learned about scalars, vectors, and matrices, which are three constructs that describe the arrangement of some values.

A single number is known as a *scalar*. More than one number arranged in a one-dimensional list (array) is known as a *vector*. More than one number arranged in a two-dimensional manner is known as a *matrix*. Visually, we can represent these three concepts as shown in Figure 8-1.

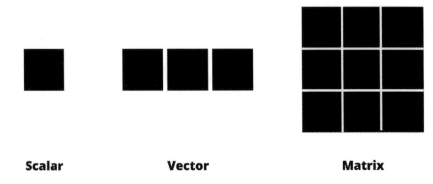

Scalar   **Vector**   **Matrix**

Figure 8-1. *A scalar, vector, and matrix*

Technically speaking, scalars, vectors, and matrices are all tensors.

- Scalars are zero-dimensional tensors.

- Vectors are one-dimensional tensors.

- Matrices are two-dimensional tensors.

However, it is a universally accepted practice that when we have more than one number arranged in three or more dimensions, we refer to such an arrangement as a *tensor*.

We can picture a tensor in the shape of a Rubik's cube, as shown in Figure 8-2.

Figure 8-2. *A tensor*

From the picture, we can see that tensors have a great capacity for data storage, as they have *n* dimensions. The *n* here is used as a proxy for the actual number of dimensions, where *n*>=3.

To better understand the relationship between scalars, vectors, matrices, and tensors, we can depict them as shown in Figure 8-3.

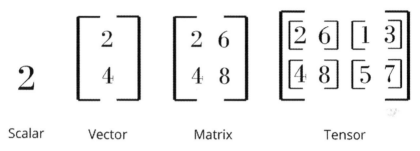

Scalar   Vector   Matrix   Tensor

Figure 8-3. *Notational representations of a scalar, vector, matrix, and tensor*

As you can see, the four data structures are quite similar to each other notation-wise as well, differing with respect to their capacity.

Although tensors usually hold numbers, they can also hold text and strings. Tensors are capable of containing large amounts of data in a compact form. This makes it easier to handle the computation of our program, even when we have enormous amounts of data that we need to use to train our machine.

Flow

The input of the program is taken in the form of tensors, which are then executed in distributed mode with the help of computational graphs. These graphs are used to set the *flow* of the entire program.

A computational graph is a flowchart of operations and functions that are needed to be carried out on the input tensor. The tensor enters on one side, goes through a list of operations, then comes out the other side as the output of the code.

This is how TensorFlow got its name—the input tensor follows a systematic flow, thus producing the necessary output.

Now that we know what TensorFlow is, let's examine how it is useful to machine learning developers.

Importance of TensorFlow

TensorFlow was mainly used for mathematical purposes. It was soon implemented in machine learning due to its high-powered computational capabilities. It made the construction of neural networks a less cumbersome task to achieve.

As the earlier definition states, TensorFlow is extremely flexible in operability and works well for machine learning algorithms across a range of platforms, like Mac OS, Windows, Linux, and Android. It was written in three languages, Python, C, and CUDA (Compute Unified Device Architecture), and although it works best with Python, it supports other languages like Java and C++.

It is also consistently revamped to keep it up to date with the constantly changing needs of programmers. Its large community is a major plus point, as this allows people who use TensorFlow to work together, help each other, and use the library effectively.

Applications of TensorFlow

Despite being relatively new, TensorFlow has already served its purpose in several areas of artificial intelligence, and continues to do so. Some of its applications include the following:

- **Image recognition:** Identifying objects or features from a photo or a video

- **Image classification:** Identifying and segregating objects from each other

- **Text summarization:** Condensing content into a few comprehensible words

- **Sentiment analysis:** Identifying whether a statement is positive, negative, or neutral

- **Speech recognition:** Recognizing and translating the spoken word into text

- **Other deep learning projects**

With TensorFlow, deep learning using neural networks becomes a piece of cake. Hence, most of the library's applications are focused on this area of artificial intelligence.

TensorFlow's Competitors

TensorFlow, although quite unique in its structure and usage, does have some competitors in the machine learning world. These are alternative frameworks that people use to perform the same functions that TensorFlow does. Some of these libraries include the following:

- Theano

- OpenCV

- PyTorch

- Apache Spark

- Keras

All these libraries, although varying in functionality and capability, have similar uses in machine learning. The Keras library can be used on top of TensorFlow to develop even more effective deep learning models. We will have the opportunity to work with Keras and TensorFlow later on in this book.

Let's now have a look at some of the advantages and disadvantages of using TensorFlow.

Advantages and Disadvantages of TensorFlow

Now that we are quite acquainted with this machine learning library, let us have a look at some of its advantages, as well as its disadvantages, when implementing it in our programs.

Advantages

Considering the number of competitors that TensorFlow has, one might wonder what the big deal is and why a lot of people regard it as their preferred deep learning library. There's a reason it stands out compared to the other libraries. We will now have a look at some of its important features in order to understand how it is advantageous for us to use it in our code.

1. It is open source. This means that it is free to access, download, use, and distribute, as per the Apache 2.0 License under which it was released. Users are not charged for implementing this library in their projects.

2. It is constantly modified. This makes room for improvements in its source code and ensures stability in its performance.

3. It can be used on multiple platforms, making it easily accessible to developers.

4. It follows the manner of abstraction, which means that all the developer needs to take care of is the overall working of the program. TensorFlow handles everything else on its own.

5. It makes data visualization much easier by providing programmers with something called a TensorBoard. This is a web-based interactive dashboard that allows us to view and observe our graphs.

6. It has several APIs in various programming languages that enable a developer to create and execute programs and graphs with ease. An example of this is the Keras API, which, as mentioned earlier, we will be using later on in this book.

7. It has a large community of enthusiastic developers, which allows TensorFlow users to connect, learn, share, and help one another.

Now, I know, this all sounds great. It almost sounds like TensorFlow is one of the greatest inventions of all mankind, doesn't it? Yet, it is quite astonishing to know that while TensorFlow gained a worldwide fan following, it also began to gain a considerable number of "haters"— developers who were mildly or greatly disappointed with the library due to some of its drawbacks.

Disadvantages

Nothing is perfect, and no matter how flawless this library might seem, it does have certain areas where it either fails or proves to be insufficient for developers. Let's take a look at some of the disadvantages of TensorFlow that were discovered by its users over the years.

1. It followed "lazy" execution. This means that the developer had to first initialize variables, and then run separate sessions for the program. This proved to be tedious for developers who had to keep opening and running sessions for even the smallest sections of their programs.

2. The TensorFlow framework was such that codes that had a very minimalistic structure still required plenty of extra lines of code.

3. The error messages were not always accurate and were sometimes faulty or incorrect, which made debugging quite a task.

4. It was slightly more complex than necessary, which made it confusing for beginners to learn, especially if they were new to computer programming in general.

Most programmers managed to work around these challenges in order to accomplish their machine learning goals, which is why TensorFlow retained a very large user base. However, the TensorFlow team soon understood that there was a lot of room for improvement in the library, in order to make it even more convenient for programmers to use.

Thus, they came up with a newer, better version—TensorFlow 2.0. It was first released as a test version, which was available for users to install, work with, and provide feedback about. Later, in 2019, TensorFlow 2.0 was officially released for people to use.

That said, let us first get a little familiar with TensorFlow 1.0, and then we'll dive into its upgraded version. We'll start by learning how to install the TensorFlow 1.0 library onto our systems.

Installing TensorFlow

One of the easiest methods of installing TensorFlow is by employing the "pip install" method. It is usually recommended because of how quick and simple it is.

Before getting into this method, let us first have a look at what "pip" is.

Getting to Know "pip"

In Python, "pip" is nothing but a standard package manager. It is used for the installation and handling of packages and software in Python, from the default source of Python packages—the Python Package Index (PyPI).

It was first released in 2008 under the name pyinstall, as an alternative to easy_install. Later, it was shortened to pip, which is supposed to be an acronym for "Pip Installs Packages."

The "pip install" Method

The general command to install a package using pip is as follows:

```
pip install <package name>
```

That's it! Just a single line. Once a package is installed using pip, it remains in the working environment until we uninstall it. This means that we don't have to keep reinstalling the package every time we want to use it within our program.

Other Useful pip Commands

Apart from installing packages, there are several commands under pip that we can call and execute in order to manage our packages conveniently. Some of these include the following:

1. `pip list`: This provides us with a list of all installed packages.

2. `pip show <package name>`: This provides us with information about the specified package.

3. `pip list—outdates`: This shows a list of all outdated packages on our system.

4. `pip search <package name>`: This searches for the specified package.

5. `pip uninstall <package name>`: This uninstalls a package from the environment.

Using "pip install" to Install TensorFlow

The great thing about this method is that we don't need to do much. All we need to do is type in a single line of code, and everything else happens on its own.

To install TensorFlow into our environment, follow these steps:

1. After opening Anaconda, make sure that you are in the correct environment, and not in the base (root) environment. For example, here I have chosen to work in myenv, as shown in Figure 8-4.

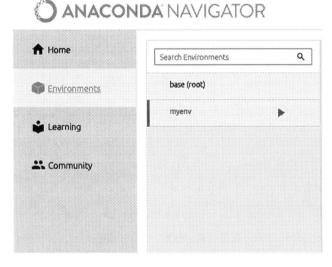

Figure 8-4. *Entering the correct environment*

2. Open the Jupyter Notebook application by launching it from within the working environment, as shown in Figure 8-5.

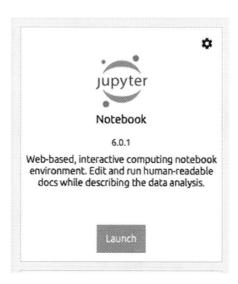

Figure 8-5. *Launching Jupyter Notebook*

3. From the dashboard, click on "New," and then select the option to open a new Python 3 Notebook, as shown in Figure 8-6.

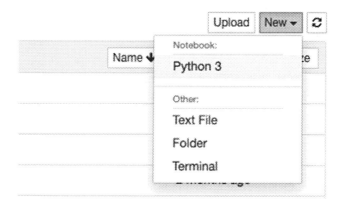

Figure 8-6. *Opening a Python 3 Jupyter Notebook*

4. In the code cell that appears, type in the following line of code to instruct the computer to begin installing TensorFlow using pip:

```
pip install tensorflow
```

The installation will begin. You will see a box appear beneath the code cell, displaying a plethora of content, representing all that is happening behind the scenes of our single-line code. An asterisk will appear at the left corner of the code cell, indicating that the code is still running. It will disappear once the process is completed, as shown in Figure 8-7.

Figure 8-7. *Installing TensorFlow*

5. When the installation is complete, we can check and see if TensorFlow is properly installed or not. To do this, first restart the kernel. Then, type in the following:

```
import tensorflow as tf
```

This small piece of code is used to call the TensorFlow library into Jupyter Notebook. The `tf` is assigned as a type of nickname for the library (we will see more of this in the next chapter when we practice coding with TensorFlow).

The cell should be executed without any errors, as shown in Figure 8-8.

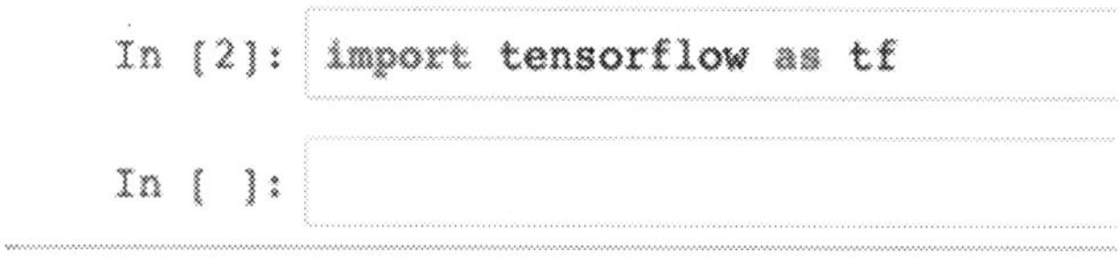

```
In [2]:  import tensorflow as tf

In [ ]:
```

Figure 8-8. *TensorFlow installed on the system*

If your notebook doesn't show any indication of an error when running the command, then congratulations! You have successfully installed TensorFlow in your Python environment.

TensorFlow also has a feature that provides users with all the necessary tools required to visualize data easily. This is known as the TensorBoard.

TensorBoard

The TensorBoard is, according to the official TensorFlow website, "TensorFlow's visualization toolkit."

It is an interface that can be used to obtain a clearer understanding of our data and our deep learning models with the help of visualization techniques.

Some of its applications include the following:

1. Visualizing parameters and metrics

2. Visualizing the computational graph

3. Viewing plots and graphs

4. Displaying media items like pictures, text, or audio

When you run TensorBoard, it will look something like Figure 8-9.

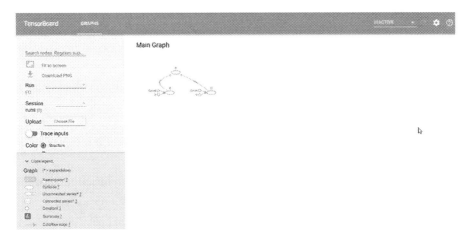

Figure 8-9. *A sample of the TensorBoard*

Figure 8-9 shows the TensorBoard panel for a very simple graph. The dashboard tabs at the top of the screen vary, depending on the components of the model. Here, we have only a single dashboard; i.e., the Graph dashboard. Now, have a look at Figure 8-10.

Figure 8-10. *TensorBoard's various tabs*

This navigation bar shows three other tabs: Scalars, Distributions, and Histograms. Each of these leads to the corresponding dashboard view, which can be used to study and improve the deep learning model.

Exploring the TensorBoard Dashboards

There are several different types of dashboards that we can access and use for their respective purposes. Let's have a look at them.

Scalars:

This shows us the changes occurring to metrics like loss and accuracy during each epoch of the training. It also allows us to keep track of the different scalar values. Being able to compare these metrics allows us to figure out any issues present within the model in order to improve it.

Graphs:

This shows us the computational graph of our model. By inspecting the graphical representation of our model, we can easily check its accuracy and reliability. This makes it easier to debug the code or make changes in its structure, thus improving the quality of the model.

Distributions:

This shows us how the inputs are distributed throughout the training of a model. It helps us to keep a visual check on the values of the weights and biases as they change over time. These parameters are extremely important when training a model, so being able to get a clear understanding of them is necessary.

Histograms:

Just like the Distributions dashboard, this helps us to keep a visual check on the values of weights and biases, but from a three-dimensional point of view, with the help of histograms. These histograms represent the changing data corresponding to the timeline of the training, enabling us to decide if any alterations need to be made to the model.

Projector:

This is used to visualize high-dimensional word embeddings. Embedding consists of the representation of words in numerical form in such a way that similar words have similar encodings.

Text:

This is used to visualize text data. These strings can be in the form of hyperlinks, tables, and so on.

Image:

This is used to visualize image data. These images are saved as .png files.

Audio:

This is used to visualize audio data. It can embed audio in the form of playable audio widgets.

Thus, with the help of the TensorBoard, we can easily inspect, modify, and verify the working of our model.

TensorBoard has also added a new service that mainly aids collaborative projects, allowing people to share their machine learning projects for free. This service is called TensorBoard.dev.

TensorBoard.dev

TensorBoard.dev allows users to host their projects online, keep track of them, and share them with others. It is free, readily available, and great for when different people from various parts of the world need to work together online.

Its benefits include the following:

1. It enables users to share their programs on a large scale.

2. It allows users to ask for help in case of any bugs or errors that they are unable to solve on their own.

3. It gives people the ability to share insights and research with others.

4. It is interactive, which helps others to have a better understanding of the model.

5. There is no requirement for any installation procedures. All it needs is a sharable link.

6. Free storage is provided, with a current limit of 10 million data points per user.

TensorBoard.dev thus makes it a less tedious task to seek help from others or contribute to other people's machine learning projects.

Note All data that is uploaded to TensorBoard.dev is publicly visible to anyone and everyone. Thus, we need to **be cautious while sharing information online**. For example, personal information, user-specific authentication codes, and so on must be avoided or hidden before releasing the program.

Summary

In this chapter, we have learned about TensorFlow, which is one of the top machine learning libraries used in Python. We have seen what it is, how it was developed, why it is important to a programmer, and how it works. We have recognized its competitors in the machine learning world, its special features that make it stand out, as well as its disadvantages so far.

We then got introduced to pip, and we learned how to install TensorFlow with the help of this package managing tool and then verify that the installation was done without any errors.

We finally had a brief overview of the TensorBoard and its features, which comes in handy while visualizing our models. We also had a look at the TensorBoard.dev tool, which allows us to share our machine learning projects easily and free of cost.

Now that we have some idea of what we are going to be working with, we can begin exploring the various features of the TensorFlow library to see how we can use it within Python, in Jupyter Notebook, for our machine learning experiments.

Additional Information

For more information on TensorFlow, check out the following information.

TensorFlow Dev Summit

The TensorFlow Dev Summit is a huge event in which developers from across the globe come together to discuss, learn, and share with one another.

The developers spend time engaging in interactive demos, technical talks, conversations with the TensorFlow team, and discussions with the TensorFlow community.

It happens every year at a location specified on the official website. Those who cannot attend the on-site summit can view it online as it is live-streamed.

The registration is free of charge. The attendee will have to bear any expenses (such as travel and stay) on their own.

More details are available on the official TensorFlow website for anyone who is interested.

TensorFlow Blogs

The TensorFlow team maintains a blog that provides users with useful updates, important changes, new additions, and so on. It also has a wide range of tutorials on various kinds of programs that machine learning enthusiasts can try on their own, or even use as a base reference to develop something new.

The articles that are published fall under the following main topics:

- **TensorFlow Core:** It deals with Python coding using Keras APIs. It is useful for beginners as well as experts.

- **TensorFlow.js:** It deals with coding using JavaScript.

- **TensorFlow Lite:** It deals with using machine learning models on IoT devices and mobile phones.

- **TFX (TensorFlow Extended):** It deals with moving models from the research phase to the production phase.

- **Swift:** It deals with developments and tutorials in Swift, which is a next-gen deep learning platform.

- **Community:** It deals with projects and experiments done by the TensorFlow community on a global scale.

Apart from their blogs, they also have a monthly newsletter that brings all the important announcements right to our inbox.

The TensorFlow Developer Certificate

The TensorFlow Developer Certificate is a great resume-boosting asset to have. It indicates the level proficiency a person has in the area of machine learning for artificial intelligence using TensorFlow.

When a person passes the assessment, they get an official certificate, as well as badges, which they can add to their professional social networking profiles. They are also added to TensorFlow's Certificate Network. This increases visibility within the TensorFlow community.

It is a great way to improve our knowledge of the library, develop our machine learning skills, and establish ourselves as experts in the field. Considering that TensorFlow is a product of Google, obtaining this certificate can undoubtedly make a data scientist's resume stand out.

More information detailing the registration, cost, preparation, and so on can be found on the main website.

Quick Links

Learn more about the TensorFlow library: `https://www.TensorFlow.org/learn`

Take a look the TensorFlow Guide: `https://www.TensorFlow.org/guide/`

Explore the models and datasets developed by the TensorFlow Community: `https://www.TensorFlow.org/resources/models-datasets`

Check out the tools that are supported by TensorFlow: `https://www.TensorFlow.org/resources/tools`

Learn more about the libraries and extensions used in TensorFlow: `https://www.TensorFlow.org/resources/libraries-extensions`

TensorBoard: `https://www.TensorFlow.org/tensorboard/get_started`

TensorFlow Dev Summit: `https://www.TensorFlow.org/dev-summit`

TensorFlow Developer Certificate: `https://www.tensorflow.org/certificate`

CHAPTER 9

Programming with Tensorflow

So far, we've learned how Python can be used for lucrative machine learning with the help of its numerous libraries, which were created for just that purpose. We also know that Jupyter Notebook is a solid development environment that can be used to build and run large programs.

In this chapter, we will take a look at how to program with the help of the TensorFlow library. This chapter deals with the initial TensorFlow release (TensorFlow 1.0), just to get us familiar with how the library used to work before the major 2.0 evolution.

Now, don't fret about having to try out these programs on your own. If you are a beginner to TensorFlow, you can begin coding with the newer version, which you will learn how to do later on. The main aim of this chapter is to give you an idea of how the original TensorFlow differs from its upgrade in terms of programming ease.

We will do this with the help of four different programs that handle some important programming concepts. They are divided as follows:

Program 1: Hello World

This is the universally accepted introductory-type program that is used in the programming world. It will teach us how to program the machine to print a statement.

© Nikita Silaparasetty 2020
N. Silaparasetty, *Machine Learning Concepts with Python and the Jupyter Notebook Environment*, https://doi.org/10.1007/978-1-4842-5967-2_9

Program 2: Constants, Variables, and Placeholders

This will help us understand the significance of constants, variables, and placeholders. It is further divided into two sub-sections:

Part A: Constants and Variables

Part B: Placeholders

Program 3: Operations in a Computational Graph

This will give us a better understanding of how the computational graph works in a TensorFlow program.

Program 4: Taking Inputs from a User for a Placeholder

This will show us how to take inputs from a user, store it in a placeholder, and then use the entered value to display some required result.

So, without further delay, let's get right into it!

Importing the TensorFlow Library

The first thing we need to do is import the TensorFlow library into Jupyter Notebook. The command is as follows:

```
import tensorflow as tf
```

The tf is kind of like a nickname given to the library. This is because, as we proceed further into the program, we will need to keep referring to the library while calling its various utilities, and typing in the full name again and again can be quite tedious. We can replace tf with any other name as well, like joe or jane, but tf is the universally accepted name, so it is advisable to use that. This also makes it easier for other people who are going through the code to understand which library is being referred to.

Once we type this command into the "Code" cell and execute it, TensorFlow will be imported into Jupyter Notebook. We can now begin programming with it.

Program 1: Hello World

We all know that the most basic program we can ever learn is the "Hello World" program. We have done this before with regular Python. Let us now do it using TensorFlow in Python.

The difference between using regular Python and using TensorFlow with Python is that the code structure varies, as you will see. In regular Python, the program would be as follows:

```
h = print("Hello World")
h
```

However, in TensorFlow it gets a little more complicated because of the internal structure of the library. Here is how the program would look:

```
h = tf.constant("Hello World")

sess = tf.Session()

sess.run(h)
```

In this case, we first create a TensorFlow constant h and assign it the value Hello World. The concept of constants will be touched upon in the next program, as mentioned before.

Next, we need to create a session, which can execute an entire graph or a part of the graph. Accordingly, it will allocate resources and accommodate values and results.

We use sess as a shorter, easier version of the command tf.Session, because in larger programs we will need to keep running and closing several sessions, and it would be cumbersome to have to write the full command every time.

Now, when we execute the program, our output will appear as follows:

```
Hello World
```

If we don't create a session and try to call the variable h to print the output, we will still obtain an output, but not quite in the way that we were hoping. Instead of giving us the value of h, it will show us that h is a tensor, and it will give us a quick summary of this tensor. And that's about it. The output will be displayed as follows:

```
<tf.Tensor 'Const:0' shape=() dtype=string>
```

Now, as you've seen, we have used the tf.constant() function in our program, which defines h as a constant (rather than a variable or a placeholder). To understand the difference between constants, variables, and placeholders better, we will have a look at another program.

Program 2: Constants, Variables, and Placeholders

Many of us have heard the terms *constants, variables*, and *placeholders* thrown around quite often, especially in the programming world. That is because they play a huge role in the development of a considerable number of programs.

Before we begin using them to code, we need to know what exactly they are. They can generally be defined in the following ways:

Constants: These are values that *never change.*

Variables: These are values that *can change* throughout the program.

Placeholders: These are empty variables that are *assigned values at a later stage* in the program.

Table 9-1 lists a few ways in which they vary from one another.

Table 9-1. *The Differences Between Constants, Variables, and Placeholders*

Constants	Variables	Placeholders
They have an initial value.	They have an initial value.	They do not have an initial value.
These values never change.	These values can change.	These values can change.
The type of value does not need to be specified.	The type of value does not need to be specified.	The type of value needs to be specified.
Example: a=tf. constant(4)	Example: b=tf. Variable(5)	Example: c=tf. placeholder (tf.float32)

Note   When we say that the "type" of value does or does not need to be specified, we mean that we need not tell the program if the constant or variable is a string, a float, an integer, etc., while for a placeholder, we need to specify this.

Now that we know what constants, variables, and placeholders are, let's go ahead and use them to create a program.

Part A: Constants and Variables

In this part, we will only be incorporating variables and constants into our code. In Part B, we will learn how to use placeholders in our program. This is because the latter requires a little more explanation than the former two.

To understand the working of variables and constants in a program, we will do some simple arithmetic, as we've already seen, since it is an easy way to demonstrate these two features. It will also give us the opportunity to explore some of the arithmetic operations that are allowed in TensorFlow.

Start by defining the constant a, as follows:

```
a = tf.constant(5)
```

Next, define the variable b:

```
b = tf.Variable(6)
```

One very important thing to note here is that the 'tf.constant()' function is spelled entirely in lowercase, while the 'tf.Variable()' function is spelled with a capitalised 'V'. This is a minute detail which can cause errors in our program if not followed correctly.

Now that we have defined the constant and the variable, let's perform some calculations on them! We will begin by finding the sum of the two values. To do so, we will use the following command:

```
sum = tf.add(a,b)
```

This is the same as typing the following:

```
sum = a + b
```

When we execute both, we will get the same output.

Now, let's say we want to change the value of our variable b. We can do so as follows:

```
new = tf.assign(b,4)
```

The tf.assign() function allows us to assign a new value to a variable. If we try to use this on a constant, it will give us an error. Here, within the brackets, we first enter the variable that we would like to change, followed by the value that we would like to change it to. We save this entire update under the variable new.

The reason for saving it under the variable new is that it cannot just get executed on its own. We need to run this code line within a session, and only then will it be executed. Thus, we store it under a variable and then call it within a session.

One very important point to be noted is that, when we are using variables, *we need to initialize them before we can begin using them in sessions*. This seems like an unnecessary step at first, but when we try to work with our variables without initializing them, our program gives us an error. We initialize the variables as follows:

```
init_op = tf.global_variables_initializer()
```

This init_op is a node, or an operation, that needs to be executed in order to initialize the variables. We can give it any name, of course, but for the sake of readability, we will use one of the conventional names for it.

Now that we have declared this, we will need to run this within a session. Let's create our session, like we did in the previous section:

```
sess = tf.Session()
```

Let's now run our init_op within the session, like so:

```
sess.run(init_op)
```

Great! Our variables have been initialized. We can now proceed with the rest of our program. Let's first find out the result of adding a and b:

```
print(sess.run(sum))
```

We add `print` before `sess.run(sum)` so that the program directly prints the result of the addition. This reduces the commands to find the sum of the two numbers and then print it into a single line of code.

We will get the sum of a and b, like this:

```
11
```

Now, let's assign the new value to b and see how our output varies:

```
sess.run(new)
```

```
print(sess.run(sum))
```

You see the difference in output? The program has changed the value of b according to the instructions given to it, and has printed the new sum of a and b. It was possible to assign a new value to b since it was a variable, but it was not possible to do so for a, as it was a constant.

Constants and variables are of great use when we have plenty of data that needs to be received, declared, stored, and called later on in the code. As we get into hardcore machine learning, we will see how they are used in a program to effectively develop and train models.

Placeholders, as mentioned earlier, require a little more explanation as to how they are implemented into a piece of code. We will see this in the next part.

Part B: Placeholders

The main idea behind placeholders is to help programmers who need to train huge models with massive amounts of data. The reason is, all this data cannot be accessed at once (unless the programmer is willing to risk having their computer crash). Thus, with the help of placeholders, this data can be accessed little by little, until it is entirely processed.

Placeholders don't need to be given an initial value, unlike constants and variables. All we need to do is specify what *type* of value we want to store in it.

Let's try initializing our first placeholder:

```
p = tf.placeholder(tf.float32)
```

Here, we are specifying that the placeholder will be holding a value that is of type `float`. This prepares the program so that at runtime it will accept a floating point number into the placeholder.

Now, let's enter our equation. This time, we will go for basic multiplication. We will enter the code as follows:

```
prod = p*2
```

Now, if we try to execute this by running it in a session, we will not get any output, because p has no value in it. We need to assign some value to p first.

Here, unlike for variables, we cannot just use `tf.assign()` to give the placeholder a value. We need to follow a different method. This involves the use of a dictionary, which we will be using to feed a value into our placeholder p.

We will first assign a single value to p, like this:

```
sess.run(prod, feed_dict={p:4.0})
```

When we execute this line of code, we will get an output like this:

8

By running this code, two things happen:

1. First, the value that we have provided (in this case, 4.0) is assigned to the placeholder p.

2. Second, the operation prod is carried out, which uses this placeholder p and its newly assigned value to produce a result.

Let's try feeding more values into our placeholder.

```
sess.run(prod, feed_dict={p:[6,7,8,9]})
```

This gives us an output for each value assigned.

We can even create a dictionary first and then feed that into our placeholder. We will demonstrate this with the help of a multi-dimensional array. First, let's define our dictionary d with some values, like this:

```
d = {p:[[0,2,4,6,8], [1,3,5,7,9], [11,15,17,19,25]]}
```

Now, we can feed these values into the placeholder p, like this:

```
sess.run(prod,feed_dict=d)
```

When we execute this line of code, we will get the product of each element of the dictionary when multiplied by 2.

Now, take a look at the next program:

```
g = tf.placeholder(tf.float32)

h = tf.placeholder(tf.float32)

sum = g+h

prod = sum*5

sess = tf.Session()

sess.run(prod, feed_dict={g:[2], h:[3]})
```

Interesting, right? Here's what happened in this program:

1.   We declared two placeholders, g and h.

2.   We then declared a variable sum that adds the values of g and h.

3.   After that, we declared a variable prod that takes the value of sum and multiplies it by 5.

4.   Finally, we ran prod in a session and fed values to g and h because sum, which is the only variable declared under prod, requires values for g and h in order to obtain a value of its own.

That's about it for placeholders! In this way, placeholders can be used to allocate an area of the graph to some value that will be fed into the program later on. It is mainly useful for when certain characteristics of the data are unknown to the programmer at the beginning of the program. For example, the programmer may not know the quantity of data that she or he will be using.

That was quite interesting, wasn't it? You can play around with variables, constants, and placeholders as well. Have a go at using them to write some small pieces of code, and see what you come up with.

In the next program, we will have a look at the architecture of computational graphs in TensorFlow.

Program 3: Operations in a Computational Graph

So far, we've learned that TensorFlow works with the help of a computational graph. This graph consists of all the variables that we declare, all the operations that we carry out, and so on. It basically works behind the scenes of a program. In TensorFlow, every node of the graph is known as an operation, even if it is just a command that initializes a variable.

We will begin by acquiring the "default graph," like this:

```
graph = tf.get_default_graph()
```

Now, let's try to retrieve the operations from within this graph:

```
graph.get_operations()
```

We will get an output like this:

```
[ ]
```

This is because we've not carried out any operations yet, so the graph has nothing to display.

We will now begin adding some nodes to this graph. Let us use some of the simple commands we have learned so far, like the following:

- Creating a constant a
- Creating another constant b
- Finding the sum of a and b as c
- Finding the product of c and a constant as d

We can do this as shown:

```
a = tf.constant(300, name = "a")
b = tf.constant(65, name = "b")
c = tf.add(a, b, name = "c")
d = tf.multiply(c, 10, name = "d")
```

In each line, name is used just for visualization to help us understand the concept of the computational graph. We can give each node any other name as well, but we have assigned our names to avoid confusion and to facilitate better understanding.

Let us now see how our graph looks by entering the following two lines to get the operations from it:

```
operations = graph.get_operations()
operations
```

Executing this gives us the result shown in Figure 9-1.

```
In [11]:  operations=graph.get_operations()
          operations

Out[11]:  [<tf.Operation 'a' type=Const>,
           <tf.Operation 'b' type=Const>,
           <tf.Operation 'c' type=Add>,
           <tf.Operation 'd' type=Mul>]
```

Figure 9-1. *Operations within a computational graph*

This shows us the number of nodes present in our graph. We had entered four different nodes, which are displayed here along with their names (a, b, c, and d) and their types (constant, constant, addition, multiplication, respectively). Let's add another node e to this:

```
e = tf.multiply(a, 8, name = "e")
operations = graph.get_operations()
operations
```

If we execute operations, we find that the number of nodes has increased by one, and this extra node is shown along with its name e, and its type Mul, as shown in Figure 9-2.

```
Out[13]:  [<tf.Operation 'a' type=Const>,
           <tf.Operation 'b' type=Const>,
           <tf.Operation 'c' type=Add>,
           <tf.Operation 'd' type=Mul>,
           <tf.Operation 'e' type=Mul>]
```

Figure 9-2. *Added Operation within the computational graph*

We can now run any or all of these nodes in a session, as shown below. As you can see, we have executed node a and node e:

```
sess = tf.Session()

with tf.Session() as sess:
    result = sess.run(a, e)
    print result
```

Here, we have run the session within a with block. This is a method that is used quite often, especially when multiple sessions are required. Instead of declaring the sess variable separately, and then typing the sess.run() command several times, we can just complete the entire process within a single loop.

Thus, we can see how the computational graph works. Of course, we won't necessarily need to develop this kind of program, especially in machine learning. However, in order to grasp the concept of graphs in TensorFlow, it is good to go through this.

Program 4: Taking Inputs from a User for a Placeholder

This type of program is especially good to know when it comes to creating a model to analyze data. This is because when we, as the developers, are creating our program, we don't really know what kind of data is going to be submitted by the user. However, we need to make sure that our program can take the user's input, perform the necessary calculations on it, and then produce the required output.

In this program, we first create two placeholders, a and b. We then declare that c is equal to some value in the form of an equation that requires a and b. After that, we say that A will be the variable name of the input that is to be assigned to a, and B will be the variable name of the input that is to be assigned to b. Finally, we create a dictionary d in which a acquires its value from A and b acquires its value from B. We then run the session to find the value of c.

This will all make a lot more sense once we actually type in and execute the code. That said, let us begin with the program:

```
a = tf.placeholder(tf.float32)
b = tf.placeholder(tf.float32)

c = (a*2) + b + 10

A = input("Enter a value for a: ")
B = input("Enter a value for b: ")

d = {a:A, b:B}

with tf.Session() as sess:
    result = sess.run(c, feed_dict = d)
    print result
```

Now when we execute this entire program, we will get the option to submit a value for A and B. These values are fed into the program and computed, and then the result of the equation is displayed.

Task Time   Keep executing this program to change the values of a and b, and see how the value of c changes accordingly. Try altering the equation for c as well, and see what happens.

Closing the Session

When I was new to using the TensorFlow library, I would practice running different kinds of code, just to get more comfortable with it. This meant that I would open several sessions in a day to execute the various commands. It was only later, however, that I learned the importance of closing a session.

We close sessions in TensorFlow mainly to free up resources and to reduce the unnecessary use of computational power. We use the following command to do so:

```
sess.close()
```

This tells the system that our session is over, so it no longer needs to compute anything. If we run our session inside a with block, however, we need not worry about having to add this extra line, as the session closes on its own once it reaches the end of the block.

And with that, we have covered some of the basics of programming with TensorFlow 1.0!

Summary

As we programmed, we perhaps noticed that some parts of the code seemed a little, well, unnecessary, right? For example, we need to keep opening (and then closing) sessions. Or, we need to initialize our variables before we can use them. Well, we can't blame the developers of TensorFlow—they did a pretty good job with creating the library in the first place. But soon even they realized that the library can be improved a little more to make the task of coding with TensorFlow even more simple for programmers.

So, what did they do?

They came up with TensorFlow 2.0.

This new version consists of updates and changes that took all the issues and inconveniences of the parent version into account. Let's dive a little deeper into this version of the library and see how TensorFlow 2.0 makes machine learning faster and easier.

CHAPTER 10

Introducing Tensorflow 2.0

TensorFlow 2.0 came as a huge blessing to the machine learning world. It was announced during the TensorFlow Dev Summit of 2019. At the time, it was still in its alpha version. Despite its being an unofficial release, it had already gathered quite a bit of attention from programmers, who soon realized that it was definitely a significant improvement from what it used to be.

This new version was developed so as to provide programmers with a machine learning library that is powerful, easy to implement, and convenient to use on any platform. It is meant to challenge its parent version by making programming even easier than before. It is also relatively less challenging for machine learning enthusiasts to pick up, especially if they are new to the TensorFlow library.

The newest release of TensorFlow specifically kept the challenges of the former release in mind. Some irksome features were removed, and some useful features were added. Of course, TensorFlow 2.0 is not the ultimate package—there is still plenty of room for improvement. But so far, it seems to have garnered a good amount of approval from programmers worldwide.

© Nikita Silaparasetty 2020
N. Silaparasetty, *Machine Learning Concepts with Python and the Jupyter Notebook Environment*, https://doi.org/10.1007/978-1-4842-5967-2_10

Features of TensorFlow 2.0

Since TensorFlow 2.0 was developed as a finer version of the original and not as a separate library of its own, many of its features are similar to those of TensorFlow 1.0. The two differ mainly with regard to a few areas where programmers noted certain avoidable attributes. That said, here are some key features of TensorFlow 2.0.

Eager Execution

According to the official website,

> *TensorFlow's eager execution is an imperative programming environment that evaluates operations immediately, without building graphs: operations return concrete values instead of constructing a computational graph to run later.*

In other words, iteration occurs at once, and we need not create a computational graph or run separate sessions for each command.

It has a natural and steady flow, and does not need to be controlled by a graph. It is intuitive because it ensures that the code follows the correct layout and structure. It also allows us to use regular Python debugging tools to identify and rectify any errors that may exist within the code.

This is different from TensorFlow's original "lazy" execution, where the programmer had to build a graph and run their lines of code within a session.

Introduction of Keras

TensorFlow implemented the Keras API as a powerful tool that can be used for model building. It supports eager execution and several other functionalities of TensorFlow. It is versatile, reliable, and effective in its working. It has been added to TensorFlow 2.0 for this very reason.

Keras used to be an independent package on its own, which users would download separately and use within their models. Slowly, TensorFlow added it to its framework, as tf.keras. This tf.keras sub-package was different from the main Keras package, so as to ensure compatibility and stability. Later, with the announcement of TensorFlow 2.0, the TensorFlow team stated that Keras would be the main high-level API of this version.

API Cleanup

TensorFlow has a multitude of APIs (Application Program Interface) for several different programming languages that can be used within a piece of code. These APIs are sets of tools, utilities, and systematic procedures that perform a particular action when called within a program.

Some of these APIs were considered to be deprecated—they did not seem to be very useful to programmers. Other APIs seemed to have similar functionalities and characteristics. Thus, while developing TensorFlow 2.0, the team decided to do some spring cleaning in this section.

Many of the APIs have therefore either been removed, replaced, or collected under a single sub-package.

Removal of Global Variables

In the previous version of TensorFlow, variables needed to be initialized before they could be used in a session. This was done with the help of the tf.global_variables_initializer() function, which would set up an operation to initialize all the variables declared in the code parallelly.

You might remember doing this in the previous chapter, where we entered a line of code like this:

```
init_ops = tf.global_variables_initializer
```

After this, we opened a new session, ran `init_ops`, and then proceeded to run the rest of our variables.

In TensorFlow 2.0, all the namespaces and mechanisms that were used to keep track of variables have been removed. Variables no longer need to be initialized before running them. They can be used directly as and when required.

Better Deployment Capabilities

TensorFlow has always provided users with the ability to work across several platforms and languages in order to develop and train models easily. TensorFlow 2.0 brings better compatibility and stability for this.

A fully trained and saved model can either be integrated directly into the application that we are working on, or deployed with the help of some important libraries, including the following:

- **TensorFlow Serving**, which enables us to implement models over HTTP/REST or gRPC/Protocol buffers.

- **TensorFlow Lite**, which enables us to implement models for mobile devices like Android or iOS, and embedded systems like the Raspberry Pi.

- **TensorFlow.js**, which enables us to implement models for JavaScript environments.

- **Additionally**, TensorFlow provides support for other programming languages like C, Java, Julia, and so on.

Powerful Experimentation Tools

Researchers can easily carry out their experiments with the help of TensorFlow 2.0, which allows them to actualize their ideas without having to compromise on speed and effectiveness.

We already learned that Keras has been added as a central high-level API to TensorFlow. Keras and similar APIs have been added to make the process of model building, improving, and training even faster and better. In fact, low-level APIs and high-level APIs work together for extra efficiency.

It is also easier to control gradient operations. Some extensions have been added as well to boost the research capabilities of the library.

Increase in Productivity

TensorFlow initially gained its fame because it effectively assisted machine learning developers and escalated their productivity. Its features and provisions greatly benefitted programmers. It saved them time and reduced their effort, while simultaneously helping them to achieve more.

TensorFlow 2.0, having upgraded from that, further increases productivity. It provides for intuitive debugging, immediate computation, scalability, and simplicity. It is also relatively easier to learn, especially for beginners.

TensorFlow 2.0 is most certainly a powerful, substantial, and robust upgrade to its predecessor. However, considering the fact that experienced artificial intelligence enthusiasts have been using TensorFlow 1.0 for a long time now, transitioning over to the newer version does provide many challenges.

Some have been debating whether TensorFlow 2.0 is really a boon or a bane. While they agree that the upgrade has its benefits, they also acknowledge that it will not be so easy for people to adapt to it, especially if they have already built working machine learning models. Also, adjusting to the new syntax can prove to be a slight obstacle, which people might feel to be unnecessary.

Let's have a look at Table 10-1, which lists some of the arguments that have been put forward as the advantages and disadvantages of TensorFlow 2.0.

Table 10-1. *TensorFlow 2.0 Pros and Cons*

Pros	Cons
It is much easier to learn compared to TensorFlow 1.0, due to its easy flow and simplified structure. Thus, people who are absolutely new to the TensorFlow library will find themselves learning it in no time.	Those who have already mastered TensorFlow 1.0 will have to unlearn it in order to understand and work effectively with TensorFlow 2.0.
It is very similar to the regular Python programming language. This means that a Pythonist will not have to worry about learning too many extra commands in order to program with TensorFlow.	Any code written with TensorFlow 1.0 that contains sessions in it will not work smoothly in TensorFlow 2.0. It can only be run in the previous version.
Since many of the APIs have been consolidated, a large part of the code that used higher-level APIs, like Keras, can still work, without having to change it.	If the code needs to be run in 2.0, it will have to be either rewritten manually or converted using the upgrade tool provided by the library.

Despite all this debate, we know that we need to make room for change, especially if it is for the better. The cons, although present, are not significantly disadvantageous to programmers. They are only minor inconveniences that can be worked around easily.

Code Comparison

So far, we have only read about the various characteristics of TensorFlow 2.0. It's functionality will make more sense once we begin actually programming with it. As mentioned already, the two versions vary with respect to writing code. In this section, we will compare both versions and see how the code differs.

We will mainly discuss five areas in which we see a significant difference:

1. The tf.print() function

2. Lazy execution vs. eager execution

3. Removal of the tf.global_variables_initializer()

4. No placeholders

5. The @tf.function decorator

For each of these areas, we will take a look at some small examples as well. In this way, we should be able to get a clear idea of how the programming style varies with each version.

The tf.print( ) Function

TensorFlow 2.0 has introduced a command that is very much similar to the print command in regular Python. In TensorFlow 2.0, we can use the tf.print() function in a single line of code to display any statement or characters of our choice.

Its usage is as follows:

```
tf.print( <string or variable to be printed> )
```

TensorFlow 1.0

In TensorFlow 1.0, it was not this easy to print anything. It required a few extra steps, as shown here:

```
import tensorflow as tf

h = tf.constant("This is a TensorFlow 1.0 program")

sess = tf.Session()

print(sess.run(h))

sess.close()
```

See how that was done? We had to declare h, state that it is equal to the given constant, which is the sentence we want to print out, open a session, run h in that session, print it, and then close the session.

So what about TensorFlow 2.0?

TensorFlow 2.0

```
import tensorflow as tf

h = tf.constant("This is a TensorFlow 2.0 program")

tf.print(h)
```

In fact, let's go a step further and make this even easier:

```
import tensorflow as tf

tf.print("This is a TensorFlow 2.0 program")
```

See how quick that was?

Thus, in TensorFlow 1.0, the program would require us to declare our string as a constant, create a session, and then execute it in the session in order to print out the string. In TensorFlow 2.0, however, all we need to do is define a variable for the string and then type in the command tf.print(), which will display the output. We can even just directly print out what we want without assigning it a variable name.

This is how TensorFlow 2.0's eager execution differs from TensorFlow 1.0's lazy execution. We can observe this in greater detail next.

Lazy Execution vs. Eager Execution

TensorFlow 1.0 followed lazy execution. It would not execute code immediately. Instead, it would wait for the particular node of the graph to be executed within a session, and only then would it run.

An example is shown next, where we have a code to print "Hello There," to find the sum of 90 and 7, and to display the value of a variable that is declared to be 300.

TensorFlow 1.0

```
import tensorflow as tf

a = tf.constant("Hello There")

b = 9+70

c = tf.Variable(300)

init_op = tf.global_variables_initializer()

sess = tf.Session()

print(sess.run(init_op))

print(sess.run(a))

print(sess.run(b))

print(sess.run(c))
```

TensorFlow 2.0

In TensorFlow 2.0, lazy execution was replaced with eager execution. This means that the code is now executed directly. There is no need to first build a computational graph and then run each node in a session. Each line of code executes immediately.

We can see this here, where we write the same code as before, but using TensorFlow 2.0:

```
import tensorflow as tf

a = tf.constant("Hello There")

b = 9+70

c = tf.Variable(300)

tf.print(a)

tf.print(b)

tf.print(c)
```

As you can see, the first set of code followed a lazy manner of execution, using a distributed graph, while the second set of code did not. It followed an eager manner of execution instead. The second code is also shorter than the first code, as it doesn't have so many steps.

Removal of tf.global_variables_initializer( )

Take a closer look at the program that we just saw. I mentioned that we skipped a few steps, right? One such step is the addition of the function `tf.global_variables_initializer()`, which we have not used at all.

The reason is that, as stated earlier, in TensorFlow 2.0 we don't need to initialize our variables. After defining the variables, we can directly begin using them within our program.

Just to get a clearer picture, let's take a look at some code to declare a variable and then display it in TensorFlow 1.0.

TensorFlow 1.0

```
import tensorflow as tf

v = tf.Variable(8)

init_op = tf.global_variables_initializer()

sess = tf.Session()

sess.run(init_op)

print(sess.run(v))
```

Simple, right? Now, let's have a look at the same code when written in TensorFlow 2.0.

TensorFlow 2.0

```
import tensorflow as tf

v = tf.Variable(8)

tf.print(v)
```

The output is the same, but the procedure is so much shorter. As a matter of fact, the number of code lines is reduced by half. And, here, we did not have to initialize the variable v. We were able to directly assign a value to it.

Speaking of variables, remember that in a previous chapter, we learned about another concept called placeholders? Well, the TensorFlow team decided that they were not going to keep placeholders in the upgrade, and thus they did away with them. We will read more about this in the next section.

No Placeholders

We already know that a placeholder is nothing but a variable to which we can assign a value at a later stage of the program. This means that, unlike variables, placeholders do not require an initial value. In TensorFlow 1.0, placeholders were used as a result of the version's lazy style of execution, as we might remember from the program in the previous chapter. However, with TensorFlow 2.0's eager execution, placeholders are not required. This is because operations are created and then evaluated immediately.

As a quick recap of how placeholders were used in TensorFlow 1.0, we will go through a small example. Let us consider a program in which we declare a constant a, a placeholder b, and an equation c consisting of a and b. We then assign the number 3 to the placeholder b using the `feed_dict` command. Finally, the values of a and b are fed to c in order to obtain the result of the equation.

TensorFlow 1.0

```
import tensorflow as tf

a = tf.constant(5)

b = tf.placeholder(tf.float32)

c = a*b

sess = tf.Session()

sess.run(print(c, feed_dict = {b : 3})

sess.close()
```

Now, when we use TensorFlow 2.0, we don't have to create any placeholders. We can directly define the constant a, variable b, and equation c, and then print the value of c. When we define c as the product of a and b, the code automatically computes the values of a and b and then stores it in c. Next, when we print c, it displays the result of the computation. The execution of the program thus becomes much faster, as we can see next.

TensorFlow 2.0

```
import tensorflow as tf

a = tf.constant(6)

b = tf.Variable(2)

c = a*b

tf.print(c)
```

See how easy the program has become? It's almost similar to a regular Python program. And we need not worry about first setting up a placeholder, then feeding data into it, and finally executing some code with it. Everything is done quickly and instantly.

@tf.function Decorator

We know that, since TensorFlow 2.0 follows eager execution, there is no need to create a computational graph first, followed by a session to run our program. Does this mean that we can no longer run a program in a distributed manner?

Not at all. We can still carry out a distributed execution for our program. All we need to do is write that piece of code in the form of a function, and then use the @tf.function decorator as a prefix to the code. TensorFlow will then understand that the code is meant to be executed in a distributed manner, and it will proceed to do so.

Let's see this in an example. Here, we first initialize values for x, y, and z. We then create a function result in which we find a, which is the sum of the three values, and we return the value of a as the output of the function. After this, we declare b, which calls the function result, supplies it with inputs as the given values of x, y, and z, and assigns the outcome of this computation as the value of b to be displayed. Finally, we once again declare b, but this time, when we call the function result, we supply it with new values for x, y, and z, allow the function to compute this result, and then feed it to b to be displayed.

Don't worry if none of that made sense to you. The code is much easier than it sounds, as you will see next.

TensorFlow 2.0

```
import tensorflow as tf
x = 7

y = 8

z = 9

@tf.function
def result(x,y,z):
        a = x+y-z
        return a

b = result(x,y,x)

tf.print(b)

b = result(1,7,3)

tf.print(b)
```

As you may have already noticed, the function here is decorated with tf.function, which allows it to be executed like a graph.

> **Note**   We are not showing any TensorFlow 1.0 code here because we do not need this decorator in it. It is only required in version 2.0.

So, from what we have just seen, it is easy to understand that there has been quite an upgrade from what TensorFlow used to be. Although it will take a little getting used to, once developers succeed in making the transition from TensorFlow 1.0 to TensorFlow 2.0, they will be able to achieve their machine learning requirements faster and more efficiently.

Now, for those who have been in the machine learning field for a considerable amount of time, it is highly likely that they have been using TensorFlow 1.0 over the past few years, which means that they might have even painstakingly developed several codes with the help of this library. Therefore, moving over to TensorFlow 2.0 may not sound very appealing, because they would have to figure out how to recreate all their code in the newer version.

Not to worry! The TensorFlow team has already thought about this and developed a pretty feasible solution. They have provided a full migration guide to help programmers make a smooth transition from 1.0 to 2.0.

They have also come up with the tf_upgrade_v2 upgrade script, which helps in automatically making the necessary changes. This reduces the amount of time and effort required by the programmer to convert their code to TensorFlow 2.0.

In the next section, we will have a look at this upgrade tool to see how it works and how it can be used in our code.

Upgrading from TensorFlow 1.0 to 2.0

The Google Brain team that developed TensorFlow knew that many machine learning programmers would have already developed several programs using TensorFlow 1.0. It would be a huge pain to have to rewrite these programs in TensorFlow 2.0, especially because the upgraded version is immensely different from its parent version. There is also scope for plenty of errors in such a process.

This is why they came up with a way to help developers migrate from TensorFlow 1.0 to TensorFlow 2.0. It makes use of the tf_upgrade_v2 function.

Note   If you are a beginner in TensorFlow, you may not have any code to upgrade, in which case you can skip this section and move ahead to the next chapter, where you will learn how to program with TensorFlow 2.0.

The tf_upgrade_v2 Upgrade Script

This utility was created to help developers in their transition from TensorFlow 1.0 to TensorFlow 2.0 by making it easier, potentially seamless, and much more convenient than manually converting the code from one version to another. It is automatically installed in TensorFlow 1.13 and higher, allowing developers to easily begin their transition.

The upgrade script has the following benefits:

1. It is just one line of code.

2. It is less time consuming.

3. It does most of the work for us.

4. It saves the upgraded code in a separate file, instead of overwriting the original file

5. It produces a report at the end of the upgrade process that tells the user what was done and what needs to be done.

Thus, although manually changing the code is not exactly prohibited, the upgrade script just seems like a shorter and easier path to take to reach the final goal, as we can see in Figure 10-1.

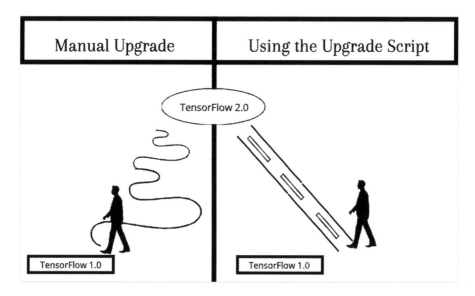

Figure 10-1. *Manual upgrade vs. the upgrade script*

Let's now have a look at how we can use this utility to transition our code.

Using the Upgrade Script

Although the name makes it sound like something very advanced that can only be attempted by professionals, it really isn't so. In fact, once we take a look at what the script is, we will be able to sigh with relief at how simple it is to follow and implement.

The structure of the script is basically like this:

```
tf_upgrade_v2 -infile < Old File Name > -outfile < New File
Name >
```

Yup! That's all it is.

The double hyphen followed by `infile` is used to call the file that contains the old TensorFlow code. In this case, it would be the name of the Jupyter Notebook that contains the code.

The double hyphen followed by `outfile` is used to rename the file that will be created when TensorFlow upgrades the code to its newer version.

Now, before we begin typing this in, we need to import TensorFlow into our Jupyter notebook. After that, we can enter this code and add our file names accordingly.

When we execute the cell, it will take a little time to perform its update, after which it will display the output. It also creates two new files:

1. A **report** about what it has done, which we can examine to check for any significant errors in the update. It mentions any keywords that have been added and arguments that have been renamed. It also recommends places where manual inspection would be preferable. All this is stored in the `report.txt` file.

2. The **new file** containing the TensorFlow 2.0 updates for which we had provided a name in the code line. This new model can be tested to ensure that it still produces the required result.

Now that we've got some idea about how this script works, let's try it out with the help of a small program. We will use the very basic "Hello World" program for this. I'm sure, by now, we all remember the code, which looks like this:

```
import tensorflow as tf

h = tf.constant("Hello World")

sess = tf.Session()
```

```
sess.run(h)

sess.close()
```

Let's say this code is in a Jupyter notebook, and this notebook is saved under the name "Hello World 1.0." To upgrade, first open a new Jupyter notebook. In the notebook, import TensorFlow 2.0, and then type in the upgrade script. The code will look like this:

```
import tensorflow as tf

tf_upgrade_v2 —infile "Hello World 1.0.ipynb"  —outfile "Hello
World 2.0.ipynb"
```

When we execute this cell, we will find the new Jupyter notebook titled "Hello World 2.0." We will also find a detailed report of the upgrade in the form of a text document called `report.txt`.

Click on the newly created Jupyter notebook. We will see that a few changes have been made. However, since this is not a very large program, not many alterations are required. The only significant change would be the modification that it makes to the `tf.Session()` line. It changes into the following:

```
sess = tf.compat.v1.Session()
```

When we open the report, it will show us the changes that it has made. For example, in this case, it will say the following:

```
INFO: Renamed 'tf.Session' to 'tf.compat.v1.Session'
```

Note   The `tf.compat.v1` module is used to allow the program to acquire TensorFlow 1.0–related functionalities, including sessions and placeholders.

Of course, when we use the upgrade script for more advanced programs, there will be many more modifications made by the script, which will all be visible in the new notebook that will be generated, as well as in the report that it creates. We would also need to make a few extra changes ourselves, since the program will not be able to do so. Overall, the upgrade script manages to do about 80 percent of the work; the rest needs to be done by us.

When using the upgrade script, there are some important points that we need to keep in mind, as follows:

1. Do not manually change the code in any way from TensorFlow 1.0 to TensorFlow 2.0. This can cause errors during the upgrade.

2. Arguments are not reordered by the upgrade script. However, keyword arguments can be added to functions in which arguments are reordered.

3. The script follows the conventional practice of importing the TensorFlow library as `tf`, and thus works accordingly.

4. The compatibility module (`tf.compat.v1`) replaces certain TensorFlow 1.0 references with those of 2.0. In any case, it is recommended that compatibility modules be removed and replaced with new APIs.

Summary

TensorFlow 2.0 seems pretty cool, doesn't it? As we have read in this chapter, it has some interesting new features that make it much more powerful and capable compared to its parent version. It does have its disadvantages, but those can easily be worked around to allow programmers to easily adapt to it.

We even compared it to TensorFlow 1.0 based on code-related differences, and we saw how much easier coding has become. Finally, we learned how we can migrate our old TensorFlow code to the newer version with the help of the upgrade script, which makes the process both smooth and quick.

TensorFlow 2.0 was mainly built to make our deep learning experiments, research, model building, and so on much more productive. In the next chapter, we will see how we can implement this library with Python to create some exciting (and fully functioning) deep learning models.

Quick Links

Read more about TensorFlow 2.0 here: `https://www.tensorflow.org/guide/effective_tf2`

Check out the Migration Guide here: `https://www.tensorflow.org/guide/migrate`

Learn more about the upgrade script here: `https://www.tensorflow.org/guide/upgrade`

Additional Information

Running TensorFlow 1.0 by Disabling TensorFlow 2.0

Although TensorFlow 2.0 is currently the default version of the library, it is still possible to access the features of TensorFlow 1.0. All we need to do is disable TensorFlow 2.0 by calling the following function:

`tf.compat.v1.disable_v2_behavior()`

This needs to be done before programming; i.e., before creating graphs, adding tensors, and so on.

Ragged Tensors

TensorFlow introduced "ragged" tensors to solve the issue of non-uniformly shaped arrays of data. For example, let's consider a set of lists of the number of letters in some words, such that each word's length varies immensely from the other, as shown here:

```
animals = tf.ragged.constant( [ ['c', 'a', 't'],
    ['h', 'i', 'p', 'p', 'o', 'p', 'o', 't', 'a', 'm',
    'u', 's'],
    ['b', 'u', 'f', 'f', 'a', 'l', 'o'] ] )
```

This will then be displayed like this:

```
<tf.RaggedTensor [ ['c', 'a', 't'],
    ['h', 'i', 'p', 'p', 'o', 'p', 'o', 't', 'a', 'm',
    'u', 's'],
    ['b', 'u', 'f', 'f', 'a', 'l', 'o'] ] >
```

Here, the first word has three letters, the second word has twelve letters, and the third word has seven letters.

We can even slice ragged tensors, the same way we would slice data in regular tensors. This is shown here:

```
print( animals [ 2 ] )
```

The outcome of this line of code would be as follows:

```
tf.Tensor(['b', 'u', 'f', 'f', 'a', 'l', 'o'], shape=(7,),
dtype=string)
```

Ragged tensors can carry out a variety of TensorFlow operations, including string operations, mathematical operations, array operations, and so on. They are also supported by many of TensorFlow's APIs, like Keras, tf.function, etc.

Non-uniformly shaped data is a common challenge that many programmers face while carrying out machine learning. Ragged tensors assist us in such situations by making the storing and processing of such data much easier.

TensorFlow Addons

TensorFlow Addons is a special-interest group created to allow users to contribute new extensions with functionalities that are not a part of the core library. It has sub-packages and sub-modules that are maintained by a dedicated team.

Some of these sub-packages include the following:

- `tfa.text`
- `tfa.image`
- `tfa.optimizers`
- `tfa.metrics`
- `tfa.callbacks`
- `tfa.rnn`

CHAPTER 11

Machine Learning Programming with Tensorflow 2.0

So far, we have learned about artificial intelligence, under which we have machine learning and its sub-set, deep learning. We have also learned about the Python programming language, which is popularly used for machine learning coding. We even got familiar with the Jupyter Notebook interface, in which we can write, edit, and debug our programs. We then saw how we can combine Python with Jupyter Notebook as an efficacious way to write our code. After this, we were introduced to the TensorFlow library as an important package within Python, and once we understood how the library was useful, we proceeded to learn about its recent upgrade—TensorFlow 2.0—which has additional features and abilities that make our machine learning models easier to build.

Now, we have finally come to the most important topic in this book: learning how to build and execute machine learning models with the help of the TensorFlow library. As explained before, the main reason TensorFlow was created was to aid developers, not just with basic machine learning programming, but also with more advanced machine learning procedures. In other words, TensorFlow was created predominantly for deep learning that employs neural networks.

© Nikita Silaparasetty 2020
N. Silaparasetty, *Machine Learning Concepts with Python
and the Jupyter Notebook Environment*, https://doi.org/10.1007/978-1-4842-5967-2_11

In this chapter, we will learn a little more about how machine learning models are made, and we will also try out seven programs of our own. Each of these programs is an image classification problem that requires neural networks, all constructed using the Keras API, which we will go through later on.

The seven programs are as follows:

1. Image Classification Using a Pre-Trained Model

2. Handwriting Recognition Using Keras in TensorFlow (Single Layer, Multi-class)

3. Clothing Classification Using Keras in TensorFlow (Multi-layer, Multi-class)

4. Clothing Classification Using Convolutional Neural Networks (Multi-layer, Multi-class)

5. Handwriting Recognition Using Convolutional Neural Networks (Multi-layer, Multi-class)

6. Image Classification for CIFAR-10 Using Convolutional Networks (Multi-layer, Multi-class)

7. Dogs vs. Cats Classification Using Convolutional Neural Networks (Multi-layer, Binary)

We will go through each of these programs step-by-step to get a thorough idea of all the processes and components involved in developing them, particularly the following:

- The structure

- The dataset

- The API

- The activation functions

- The optimizer

- The program

By fully understanding these seven programs, we will be well equipped to create our own models for other similar problems.

Before we begin programming, there are two things that we need to do to prep ourselves:

1. Understand the structure of a machine learning model.

2. Get acquainted with Keras, which we will be using under TensorFlow to build and train our deep learning models.

In Chapter 2, we saw the steps that are to be followed when solving a machine learning problem. Here, we will go through the general structure of a machine learning model to obtain a clearer idea of how it is built.

Structure of a Machine Learning Model

Machine learning, as mentioned earlier, requires part of the work to be done by us. The rest of it is all done behind the scenes by the computer. In other words, it all happens in the backend of the code. This, in all honesty, saves us, as programmers, a lot of trouble. There are, however, still plenty of tasks that we need to carry out while creating our model in order to make sure that we get the output we desire.

A machine learning developer's task is mainly to build the model and then run it. There are several components to this model, depending on what exactly we are trying to accomplish, but the general architecture remains the same.

Since we will be using neural networks to carry out our machine learning processes, we will study the structure of a deep learning model that uses a neural network. The overall idea for the structure of the model is as shown in Figure 11-1.

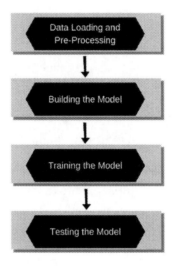

Figure 11-1. *Flowchart of a machine learning model*

As we can see in the flowchart, there are four main steps involved in developing a working machine learning model, as follows:

1. **Data loading and pre-processing:** This part accepts data, manipulates it, then prepares it for training and testing.

2. **Building the model:** This is the part where the developer specifies the various components of the model.

3. **Training the model:** This part takes the training data and begins performing calculations on it to get an optimum result.

4. **Testing the model:** This part validates or checks the accuracy of the model.

The first two steps require the time, effort, and skills of a programmer, since they involve the handling of data and the creation of a working model. For the last two steps, all the programmer has to do is set the model running and then kick back and relax while the machine does all the hard work.

Let's go through this structure in a little more detail to get a better idea of what it does, how it works, and what needs to be done.

Data Loading and Pre-Processing

In Chapter 2, we had a look at the different methods of collecting data. We also learned that this data requires some pre-processing before it can be used for any kind of analysis in order to ensure optimal results. This means that we might need to add, remove, or change some values.

Now remember, *this does not mean that we are completely changing our data*, which can result in incorrect outputs. We are just making it more readable for our system to take and work with.

Here are some examples of this:

1. Suppose we had data containing a list of 500 married women and the number of children each of them have. From this list, almost everyone has at least one child. Only five of them have no children. Now the problem is that we need to predict the number of hours of sleep these women get in a day, based on the number of children they have. Obviously, the details of these five women would not be required for this study since they do not have children. Thus, we would have to remove their data from the list.

2. Sometimes, apart from numerical values, our data may also contain terms like *None* or *No*, which could basically imply a zero, depending on the problem. Thus, we would need to either change those values to 0 or remove them from the dataset.

3. In some cases, we may want to round off our numerical values to the nearest whole number. This can be done either for the whole dataset or just for a section of it.

Data can be altered manually. Applications like spreadsheets or visualization software come in handy when working with structured data. However, when the dataset is huge, it becomes quite tiring and monotonous to work with. Thus, most developers use a Python library called Pandas, which provides users with several tools and utilities to work on their data. With the help of Pandas, users can import a `.csv` file (csv: comma separated values) from their local system into a Jupyter notebook.

In this book, we will be using image datasets that are already integrated within the TensorFlow library. They can easily be called with the help of a TensorFlow function, as we will see later on.

The data that we use for training machine learning models is divided into two categories: labels and features.

Labels: These are the components of the data that are to be predicted; i.e., the dependent variable or output. They are determined based on the features provided to the system.

Features: These are the components of the data that are used for prediction; i.e., the independent variable or input. They determine the labels of the outputs. When choosing features, it is important to ensure that they are independent and distinct.

When training a deep learning model, we can choose either of the following methods based on how we intend to input our features and labels:

- **Supervised learning:** We feed the model with the features and the labels.

- **Unsupervised learning:** We feed the model with the features only.

- **Semi-supervised learning:** We feed the model with some labeled features and some unlabeled features.

Note   The quality of the labels is proportional to that of the features. In other words, better features result in more accurate labels.

Once we have finished altering our data, we need to split it into two parts: the training data and the test data.

> **Training data:** Training data is what is fed into the model to be used while it is training. This will generally be a greater proportion of the data, since the model requires a larger amount of data when training to get more accurate results.

> **Test data:** Test data is what is fed into the model after it has finished training and settled on optimal parameters. This will generally be a lesser proportion because it is only meant to help the model determine how accurate or inaccurate its prediction is.

After we are done pre-processing the data, the next step is to build the model.

Building the Model

We need to develop the architecture of our machine learning model. In this case, we will be using a neural network. Thus, we need to arrange the neural network by defining the following:

- The number of hidden layers

- The number of neurons in each layer

- The weights and biases

- The activation function

In Chapter 3, we learned how neural networks work, and we studied their different types. For example, convolutional neural networks (CNNs) are best used for image classification and recognition, and recurrent neural networks (RNNs) are great for machine translation and speech recognition. We can choose our preferred neural network after careful consideration of our data, resources, and desired outcome, and accordingly build the model that we require.

Training the Model

Once the model is built, it is ready to be trained. This is where the programmer steps aside and gives way to the machine, which proceeds to do some intense work. All we need to do here is call the training data into the model and then start the process.

During training, the model begins trying out different values and replacing the parameters, i.e., the weights and the biases, in order to come up with the most suitable equation that will give high accuracy and low error. It follows a trial-and-error manner, and keeps changing the values of the parameters until it gets a result that is satisfactory.

We have already seen the following in Chapter 3:

- The values of the weights and biases are constantly tweaked to make the output more suitable and to give stronger predictions. This is called training the model.

- The output is predicted from the input data. This is known as forward propagation.

- The weights and biases are modified in order to reduce the loss. This is known as back propagation.

Although it seems like everything should end here, it's not always a good idea to do so.

Why?

Well, there is always a possibility that the result still may not be the most optimal one. For example, overfitting can happen, resulting in inaccuracy. This is why, after training, the model must also be tested.

Testing the Model

Once we have our trained model, we need to feed the test data into it. We then allow the model to run this data through to see how accurate its predictions are. In this way, we validate the model.

Depending on this accuracy, we can decide if we want to change certain aspects of the model and then retrain it, or leave it as it is. Of course, there are several other factors that can affect this decision as well, including time, computational power, and so on. For example, the programmer may not have enough resources to redesign and retrain the model. Or perhaps there isn't enough time. So, before retraining the model, the programmer must take all of these factors into consideration.

The machine continues to repeat this cycle of training and testing the model until it produces an acceptable outcome.

The structure of a machine learning model can vary greatly with regard to more specific factors, depending on the type of problem that we are solving. Hence, as mentioned earlier, we need to correctly define our problem and the solution we hope to achieve, and then carefully plan out our model to minimize error.

Now that we are aware of the general design of a machine learning model, the next thing we need to do is get familiar with the Keras API, which is integrated with the TensorFlow library and which we will be using to develop our code.

Keras

Before we learn about Keras as a TensorFlow API, let's have a look at Keras as an independent and popular machine learning library.

Keras is an open source deep learning library. It was written in Python and can work on top of TensorFlow, as well as on Theano, R, PlaidML, and the Microsoft Cognitive Toolkit. It was developed within the project ONEIROS (Open-ended Neuro-Electronic Intelligent Robot Operating System).

It was initially released on March 27, 2015, under the MIT license.

According to the official website, Keras mainly focuses on "Deep Learning for Humans."

In other words, the developer is its priority, rather than the machine. It was created to make the programming process less burdensome for the user. It makes it easier for the user to write and debug code, and also provides sufficient guides and documentation.

Keras was initially just an individual library that could be called and deployed within a program. In fact, its original backend was Theano. However, when Google introduced TensorFlow, programmers began to implement both together, until it became such that one could not have Keras without TensorFlow and vice versa. Seeing the growing popularity of this deadly combination, Keras soon made TensorFlow its default backend, which was a smart move on their part.

In 2017, TensorFlow added the tf.keras sub-module into its package, which was separate from the Keras library that needed to be installed (using the `pip` function). This was the first step to support Keras within its package. Finally, with the release of TensorFlow 2.0 in 2019, Keras became the official high-level API for machine learning. This gave an added boost to both the libraries, as they could now be used together to develop and train powerful neural networks.

Features of Keras

Keras contains several features and tools that make deep learning much easier. Some of these include the following:

1. It can function smoothly on CPU as well as on GPU.

2. Models can easily be exported onto servers, browsers, embedded devices, and so on.

3. It is flexible and consistent, making research and deployment less difficult for users.

4. It supports several types of neural networks, like CNNs and RNNs.

5. It has extensive documentation for further study, and a community for users to support one another.

Thus, Keras provides the user with reliable support and powerful resources that can be implemented into a program to design, train, test, and deploy deep learning models.

We now know how a machine learning model is structured. We also learned about Keras, an important API under TensorFlow that makes our coding experience much better. With this, we can go ahead and start building our very first deep learning model with TensorFlow!

We will be developing deep learning programs to segregate our data into several groups based on certain similarities. In other words, we will be solving classification problems.

We have already heard about such problems. Under classification, we have two main types: binary classification and multi-class classification.

Binary Classification

This is a very simple type of classification problem. Here, the variable to be predicted can take either one of two possible values. In other words, the data needs to be split into two groups.

Let's take a very simple example. Suppose we have a set of nine random numbers available to us: 2, 5, 700, 75654, 8273, 9, 23, 563, and 0.

We can separate these numbers into two groups:

Odd Numbers (5, 8273, 9, 23, 563)

Even Numbers (2, 700, 75654, 0)

As you can see, we have two groups or "classes" here based on the type of number. Five of the given numbers are odd, and four of them are even.

Let's take another example. Suppose we have a set like this: "doe," "ram," "stag," "ewe," "rooster," "chicken."

This can be separated out into the following:

Male ("ram," "stag," "rooster")

Female ("doe," "ewe," "chicken")

Once again, here we have two categories based on their gender, male and female, each having three variables. Each variable within the set of data is divided accordingly.

Other more advanced applications of binary classification include cancer detection (cancer present/cancer absent), spam detection (spam/not spam), etc.

Multi-class Classification

This is also called multinomial classification. Here, the variable to be predicted can take one of many possible values. In other words, the data needs to be separated into more than two groups.

For example, suppose we have a set like this: "rose," "cucumber," "tulip," "lily," "apple," "carrot," "potato," "orange," "sunflower."

We can separate them into these groups:

> *Flowers* ("rose," "tulip," "lily," "sunflower")
>
> *Fruits* ("cucumber," "apple," "orange")
>
> *Vegetables* ("carrot," "potato")

As you can see, we have three groups into which the data is divided based on type: four of the variables are flowers, three of them are fruits, and two of them are vegetables.

Let's consider another example. Take a look at this set of eleven random numbers: 9, 55, 8, 22, 27, 16, 205, 93, 4, 49, 81.

Any guesses on how we can divide them?

Yes, that's right! We can divide them into the following groups:

> Multiples of 2 (8, 22, 16, 4)
>
> Multiples of 3 (9, 27, 93, 81)
>
> Multiples of 5 (55, 205)
>
> Multiples of 7 (49)

We have four groups here based on the highest common factor (2, 3, 5, or 7): the multiples of 2 consisting of four variables, multiples of 3 consisting of four variables, multiples of 5 consisting of two variables, and multiples of 7 consisting of one variable.

Other more advanced applications of multi-class classification include eye-color recognition (blue, green, light brown, dark brown, grey), cat-breed identification (Persian, Munchkin, Bengal, Siamese, Sphynx), etc.

As we can see, in all these classification examples, the variables were grouped together depending on the characteristics that they shared. In this way, data can be classified or grouped based on similarities in particular characteristics or features.

We will now get into the seven programs that we spoke about at the beginning of this chapter. This will help illustrate all that we have discussed till now, and will give you a clearer picture of the entire concept of machine learning with the help of Python and TensorFlow, within Jupyter Notebook.

Programming with TensorFlow 2.0

The programs that we will be learning comprise image classification problems. Before we get into them, let's have a quick look at how such problems need to be dealt with in order to solve them.

Image Classification: An Overview

Image classification is one of the most popular areas of deep learning due to its vast usability in practical purposes. It is the process of separating images within a dataset into groups, based on their similar features.

For example, suppose we had images of a goldfish, a grasshopper, a sparrow, a rabbit, a penguin, a cat, a vulture, and a shark, as shown in Figure 11-2.

Figure 11-2. *Eight images of different creatures*

We can separate them into different groups, based on which class they belong to, as shown in Figure 11-3.

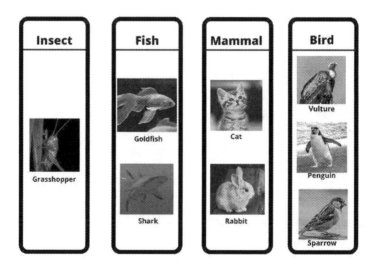

Figure 11-3. *Classifying the images*

We thus have the following four classes:

- Insect (grasshopper)

- Fish (goldfish, shark)

- Mammal (cat, rabbit)

- Bird (vulture, penguin, sparrow)

Having studied these subjects in school, we already know which of these creatures falls under which category. We can use our natural intelligence to distribute the images easily. But how would an artificially intelligent computer figure this out?

We would have to train it to understand the ways in which some of the creatures relate to each other, while others don't.

The model can be trained by feeding it with labeled pictures of different kinds of creatures. The labels would inform the machine if the image is that of an animal, a bird, a fish, or an insect. The machine would then begin to observe all the images under a single class to gather information on any kind of common features among them.

For example:

- The insects have six legs and antennae.

- The fish have streamlined bodies and fins.

- The mammals have four legs and furry bodies.

- The birds have wings and two legs each.

Once it has gathered its observations and made predictions that are verified to be accurate, it can be used for further problem solving.

Now, if we give it the eight images from Figure 11-2, it would solve the problem effortlessly and classify the images according to their type by studying each picture, finding its closest possible label match, and placing it in that class. This is how image classification is done using a machine learning model.

In the programs that we will be going through, we will focus on instructing the computer to train and test similar image classification models with the help of neural networks.

Let's start with our very first deep learning program.

Program 1: Image Classification Using a Pre-Trained Model

Before we begin building models and training them, we need to understand what our main objective is. Many times, we focus more on creating models that give us high accuracy during validation, but we completely forget to carry out a final inference to see if the model has really been trained well.

Inference is the process of using a trained machine learning model to make a prediction.

During inference, we take a random element from the entire dataset and pass it through the model to see if it can predict that element's class correctly. The result of this prediction helps us to infer or deduce whether the model is accurate or not.

To make this clearer, let's write a fun little image classification program, in which we will take a pre-trained model and carry out inference to validate its predictions.

Note   Don't worry too much about understanding each and every step of this program. As long as you get the basic idea of what is happening, that should be enough.

The Working

Since this is a model that has already been trained, we need not worry about that part. All we need to do is load an image from the file, prepare it, feed it to the model, and retrieve its outcome.

The Structure

The structure of this program is short and sweet:

1. It loads the pre-trained model into the Jupyter notebook.

2. It loads an image into the notebook.

3. It prepares the image for the model.

4. It predicts the probability across all output classes.

5. It converts the probabilities into labels.

6. It identifies the highest probability.

7. It displays the result.

The API

This program will be using the newly added high-level Keras API.

The Program

Step 1: Open a new Jupyter notebook.

Start by launching the Anaconda application. Enter the required virtual environment, and then launch Jupyter Notebook within it. From the Jupyter Notebook dashboard, open up a new notebook for Python 3 programming. We can give this notebook a name, like "Inference for Pre-Trained Models."

Step 2: Import TensorFlow and Keras utilities into the notebook.

Import TensorFlow, the Keras API, and all the extra functions into the Jupyter notebook, using the following code:

```
import tensorflow as tf
import tensorflow.keras

from tensorflow.keras.preprocessing.image import load_img,
img_to_array

from tensorflow.keras.preprocessing import image

from tensorflow.keras.applications.vgg16 import VGG16,
preprocess_input, decode_predictions

from tensorflow.keras.applications.resnet50 import ResNet50,
preprocess_input
```

Step 3: Load the model into the notebook.

We need to load the pre-trained model into the notebook. In this program, we will be trying out both VGG16 and ResNet50. To start with, let's call VGG16 into our program. We can add it to our code like this:

```
model = VGG16()
```

This will load the pre-trained model into the Jupyter notebook.

Step 4: Load an image into the notebook.

We now need to load an image into the notebook. The great thing about using this pre-trained model is that we can upload any picture that we want and then test it to see if it works correctly.

The image we will be using is that of a kitten. We can load it into our notebook, like this:

```
image = load_img('Kitten1.jpg', target_size=(224, 224))
image
```

The image will be displayed as shown in Figure 11-4.

Out[40]:

Figure 11-4. *Loading the image file*

Note   Just remember that when you are saving an image onto your computer, it's always a good idea to save it in the same folder as the Jupyter notebook that you are working in. For example, if your notebook is saved under Desktop/My Programs, you can move the image to Desktop/My Programs as well. This makes it easier for you to access it later on in your code, without the need for typing in the entire file path.

Step 5: Prepare the image for the model.

We first need to convert the image's pixels into a Numpy array, like this:

```
image = img_to_array(image)
```

We then need to reshape the array, like this:

```
image = image.reshape((1, image.shape[0], image.shape[1],
image.shape[2]))
```

Finally, we will preprocess the input, like this:

```
image = preprocess_input(image)
```

Step 6: Make the prediction.

We can now predict the probability of the image's belonging to each class. After this, we convert these probabilities into the class labels, and then retrieve the result that seems the most probable. The code for this is shown here:

```
result = model.predict(image)

label = decode_predictions(result)

label = label[0][0]
```

Step 7: Display the classification.

The model's prediction can be displayed along with its percentage probability with the help of the following code:

```
print('%s (%.2f%%)' % (label[1], label[2]*100))
```

The output will come like this:

```
        Egyptian_cat (87.00%)
```

We can see that the VGG16 model has not only predicted that the image is that of a cat, but also predicted its species; i.e., an Egyptian cat. Along with this, it has given the probability of its answer's being correct as 87 percent.

Nice, right?

Let's try this again, and this time, with a ResNet50 model.

Just change the code in Step 3 to this:

```
model = ResNet50()
```

Now repeat the remaining steps, leaving the same image file, and run the prediction. See what we get?

>Egyptian_cat (71.94%)

The ResNet50 model also gives the same prediction, but it is only 71.94 percent sure of its answer.

So, can we say that these models are perfect, because they were able to identify the image of a kitten correctly? Well, here's another example, in which I have changed my image to that of another kitten, as shown in Figure 11-5.

Figure 11-5. *Loading another image file*

Here is what the models predicted:
VGG16:

>Chihuahua (21.55%)

ResNet50:

>Pembroke (17.49%)

As we can see, one model identified my kitten as a Chihuahua, while the other model identified him as a Pembroke (which, after a bit of searching, I found out refers to the Pembroke Welsh Corgi). In short, both the models thought that my kitten was a dog.

Thus, as we learn to create, train, and validate deep learning models, we will also be required to carry out an inference on them to ensure that they have actually been trained correctly. Since they are just machines, it is not possible to get a model that is completely infallible. Our aim, however, is to get the highest accuracy with the least number of errors. Once such models are developed and approved, they can be implemented into real-world applications.

It is now time to learn how to build our very own neural networks for deep learning. In the next few programs, we will go through various types of image classifiers, and we will see how we can set them up in different ways to classify several images.

Program 2: Handwriting Recognition Using Keras in TensorFlow (Single Layer, Multi-class)

Handwriting is unique to a particular individual. You might have observed that some people have extremely neat and aesthetic handwriting, whereas others have handwriting that is almost illegible. There is also a clear distinction when writing different characters. For example, some might just put a dot over their *i*'s, while others prefer to draw a small circle. We then have differences in slant, size, thickness, and so on.

It is this uniqueness that makes handwriting recognition quite a challenge, especially for artificially intelligent machines. However, it is not impossible to train a model to figure out similarities, and thus differentiate between characters.

The Working

Images are basically grids made up of numbers. These numbers tell us the pixel value or intensity. Thus, these numbers can be manipulated to obtain the characteristics of the image. This enables us to find similar features in different images.

The Structure

The architecture of this model is as follows:

1. It loads the given dataset of images.

2. It divides the data into the training set and the test set.

3. It creates the neural network with as many layers as we specify, along with the activation function provided by us.

4. It begins training with the training data to recognize the similarities and differences between each image and segregate them accordingly.

5. It then tests its accuracy with the test data to see how well it has learned the difference between each image.

6. It carries out inference to make sure that its prediction is correct.

The Dataset

The dataset that we will be using in this program is the MNIST dataset. The full name of MNIST is Modified National Institute of Standard Technology. It is a set of handwritten digits (from 0 to 9). It is used to train models for handwriting recognition.

It is, as can be understood by the name, a modified version of the previous NIST datasets. The great part about it is that it is pre-divided into training data and test data. The training dataset consists of 60,000 images, while the test dataset consists of 10,000 images. They are all of size 28x28 pixels.

It has become a standard database that is used to practice image classification. It is tightly integrated with Keras and TensorFlow, making it readily available and easy to call into the model. It is great for teaching machine learning to beginners as the data is already manipulated and divided, making the rest of the program easy to do.

The API

We will be using the Keras API within TensorFlow, as it makes our work easier by providing us with the necessary utilities for creating our neural network.

The Activation Functions

We will be using the Softmax activation function only, since we have just a single layer.

The Optimizer

We will be using the Adam optimizer in this neural network.

The Program

Step 1: Open a new Python 3 Jupyter notebook.

We will start by opening a brand new Python 3 Jupyter notebook. We need to make sure that it is in the correct environment. We can also give it a name if we want to. Something like "My First Neural Network" or "Programming with TensorFlow 2.0" would suffice.

Step 2: Import TensorFlow into your kernel.

In the first "Code" cell that appears, we type in the following:

```
import tensorflow as tf
```

This will call the TensorFlow library into our kernel, allowing us to use it.

Step 3: Load the MNIST dataset.

We now need to call the dataset into our Jupyter notebook. We do this by typing the following:

```
data = tf.keras.datasets.mnist
(ip_train, op_train), (ip_test, op_test) = data.load_data()
```

This tells the program to call the dataset from within the library, and to load it into the kernel. As you can see, we have begun making use of the Keras API as well. `ip_train` and `ip_test` are nothing but the training and test data for the inputs. Similarly, `op_train` and `op_test` are the training and test data for the outputs.

Step 4: Prepare the data.

Now, as mentioned earlier, we need not manipulate our data too much, since that has already been done for us. However, we do need to normalize our data. This makes sure that the pixel values of the images range between 0 and 1. We do this by dividing each element of the dataset by 255, as shown here:

```
ip_train, ip_test = ip_train / 255.0, ip_test / 255.0
```

Step 5: Build the neural network.

We will now begin creating the architecture of our neural network. We start by flattening the input images (making them one-dimensional), after which we add one dense layer. This layer uses the Softmax activation function. See the following:

```
model = tf.keras.models.Sequential([
    tf.keras.layers.Flatten(input_shape = (28,28)),
    tf.keras.layers.Dense(10, activation = 'softmax')
])
```

The number of neurons in the last dense layer depends on the number of outputs (labels) that we are expecting. In this case, we expect ten outputs (the number of digits ranging from 0 to 9), and hence, the number of neurons is ten.

Step 6: Compile the model.

We compile our model by selecting the loss function, optimizer, and the metrics.

Loss function:

This measures the accuracy of the model during training. We need to minimize this function to ensure that the model is on the right path.

There are three main loss functions that we will be using:

1. binary_crossentropy: This is the default loss function that is used for binary classification.

2. categorical_crossentropy: This is the default loss function that is used for multi-class classification.

3. sparse_categorical_crossentropy: This is used for multi-class classification, without the need of using one hot encoding.

Optimizer:

Depending on the data and the loss function, the model makes changes to itself to produce the most optimal results. The optimizer is used to alter the value of the weights in order to minimize the loss function.

Metrics:

This keeps a check on the steps that the model takes doing training and testing. The "accuracy" option considers the number of images that are correctly recognized and classified.

To compile the model, we type in the code as follows:

```
model.compile(optimizer = 'adam',
                        loss = 'sparse_categorical_crossentropy',
                        metrics = ['accuracy'])
```

Here, we use the adam optimizer, the sparse_categorical_cross_entropy loss function, and accuracy metrics.

Step 7: View the model.

This is more of an optional step. We can use it to view a summary of the model's structure.

```
model.summary()
```

We will get a mini report, like in Figure 11-6.

```
In [6]:  model.summary()

         Model: "sequential"

         Layer (type)                 Output Shape              Param #
         =================================================================
         flatten (Flatten)            (None, 784)               0
         _____
         dense (Dense)                (None, 10)                7850
         =================================================================
         Total params: 7,850
         Trainable params: 7,850
         Non-trainable params: 0
```

Figure 11-6. *A summary of the model*

This report shows us the type of layers, the output and shape, and the number of parameters in each layer. We also get a count of the total parameters, along with the number of trainable and non-trainable parameters.

Step 8: Train the model.

We can now "fit" our model with the help of this line of code:

```
model.fit(ip_train, op_train, epochs = 6)
```

Fitting the model is the process of helping the model understand the relationship between its inputs, parameters, and predicted outputs so that it can make better predictions in the future.

This step begins the training. The model takes the input data and fits it through its neural network for a total of six epochs, as specified.

An epoch is one full cycle of passing the entire data through the model.

While training, the code displays the loss, as well as the accuracy (out of 1.0), as shown in Figure 11-7.

```
In [7]:  model.fit(ip_train, op_train, epochs = 6)

Train on 60000 samples
Epoch 1/6
60000/60000 [==============================] - 4s 59us/sample - loss: 0.4688 - accuracy: 0.8775
Epoch 2/6
60000/60000 [==============================] - 3s 54us/sample - loss: 0.3034 - accuracy: 0.9152
Epoch 3/6
60000/60000 [==============================] - 3s 54us/sample - loss: 0.2835 - accuracy: 0.9212
Epoch 4/6
60000/60000 [==============================] - 3s 55us/sample - loss: 0.2732 - accuracy: 0.9241
Epoch 5/6
60000/60000 [==============================] - 3s 54us/sample - loss: 0.2672 - accuracy: 0.9259
Epoch 6/6
60000/60000 [==============================] - 5s 77us/sample - loss: 0.2615 - accuracy: 0.9269

Out[7]:  <tensorflow.python.keras.callbacks.History at 0x1364ce710>
```

Figure 11-7. *Training the model through six epochs*

Step 9: Test the model.

To evaluate how good our model is, we need to test it. We use the test data this time and run it through the newly obtained parameters, using the following code:

```
model.evaluate(ip_test, op_test)
```

This runs the data through a single epoch and gives an output displaying the loss, as well as the accuracy, as shown in Figure 11-8.

```
In [8]:  model.evaluate(ip_test, op_test)
         10000/10000 [==============================] - 0s 46us/sample - loss: 0.2714 - accuracy: 0.9233
Out[8]:  [0.27139872521460057, 0.9233]
```

Figure 11-8. *Testing the model*

As we can see, the accuracy here is above 90 percent, which is quite good for a single-layer model, even if it's not 100 percent accurate.

Let's carry out inference now to see how well our model can recognize handwritten digits that are fed to it.

Step 10: Carry out inference.

To do this, we will be using two extra libraries: Matplotlib and Numpy. We won't be getting into the details of these libraries, but will just utilize a few of their functions.

Start by importing the Matplotlib library into the Jupyter notebook, like this:

```
import matplotlib.pyplot as plt
%matplotlib inline
```

Next, call the image to be tested from the MNIST dataset and save it under a variable, like this:

```
test_image=ip_test[9999]
```

The number within the square brackets can be any value from 0 to 9,999 (The total number of test images is 10,000, remember?).

Now plot the image of the selected element by entering the code, like this:

```
plt.imshow(test_image.reshape(28,28))
```

This will display the output shown in Figure 11-9.

```
In [60]:  plt.imshow(test_image.reshape(28,28))

Out[60]:  <matplotlib.image.AxesImage at 0x1360fba50>
```

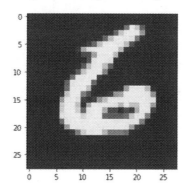

Figure 11-9. *Plotting the image*

When we look at the image, we can recognize it as the number 6. However, we need to check if the computer is able to do that as well.

Import the Numpy library, followed by the image function under Keras:

```
import numpy as np
```

```
from tensorflow.keras.preprocessing import image
```

Convert the image into a Numpy array, like this:

```
test_image = image.img_to_array(test_image)
```

Reshape the test image like this:

```
test_image = test_image.reshape(1,28,28)
```

Store the result of the model's prediction under a variable, and then call that variable to display the prediction, like this:

```
result = model.predict(test_image)
```

```
result
```

We will get an output like this:

```
array([[8.8958717e-07, 4.1242576e-14, 6.5094580e-05,
3.4720744e-09,
        4.7850153e-07, 7.9171368e-06, 9.9992573e-01,
        7.4808004e-13,
        3.1107348e-08, 2.5647387e-11]], dtype=float32)
```

Round off the array elements using the following Numpy function:

```
np.around(result)
```

We will get the rounded off values of the array, as shown here:

```
array([[0., 0., 0., 0., 0., 0., 1., 0., 0., 0.]],
dtype=float32)
```

Now, to find the element that gives the maximum value among all the elements of the array, we use the following code:

```
(np.around(result)).argmax()
```

This gives the output like this:

```
6
```

As we can see, the highest value of 1 is located in the sixth position (arrays start from 0, not 1). Thus, we can verify that the model has predicted the answer correctly.

Note   Just remember that sometimes, when you execute the "Code" cell containing your model, you may not get any error. However, when you try to run the code to train the model, an error might come up, which means you will need to go back and check your model and the parameters before you can train it.

And there we have it! We have just created our first neural network with the help of TensorFlow 2.0.

It's quite tempting to just stop here and feel thrilled that we are done. But a single-layer neural network is only the first step in deep learning. In practical applications, most neural networks require more than a single layer to get a really great result. Let's see how to build such a model in the next program.

Program 3: Clothing Classification Using Keras in TensorFlow (Multi-layer, Multi-class)

In this modern generation, clothing has become one of the top priorities for most people. When it comes to business, fashion is one very important industry, considering how much individuals are willing to invest on the kind of clothes they wear. Now just imagine what would happen if we integrated artificial intelligence with this already booming industry—the entire sector would be transformed.

It's definitely an interesting area to get into, since it has so much scope for new innovations. For now, we will get a little taste of it by building a neural network to classify images of clothing.

In this program, we will be doing pretty much the same things we did previously, but with a different dataset and a few extra layers. We will also add a few more lines of code, just to explore some new functions under TensorFlow. The general structure, API, and optimizer all remain the same or at least are similar here, so we will skip that part and go ahead to the rest of the program.

The Dataset

The dataset that we will be using for this program is the Fashion MNIST dataset.

This dataset is a part of Zalando's research images and can be used instead of the original MNIST dataset to train an image classification model.

It is a set of 60,000 training images and 10,000 test images. Each is a 28x28 greyscale image of an item of clothing. Altogether, there are ten classes in the dataset.

The Activation Functions

In this program, we will use two activation functions:

1.   ReLU

2.   Softmax

The Program

Step 1: In a new Jupyter notebook, import the TensorFlow library and Keras utilities.

```
import tensorflow as tf

from tensorflow.keras import datasets, layers, models
```

By adding this extra `import` step, we now no longer have to keep typing "tf.keras" before calling each function. We can just call it directly, as you will see in the next step.

Step 2: Load the Fashion MNIST dataset.

We can load the Fashion MNIST dataset into our Jupyter notebook like this:

```
data = datasets.fashion_mnist
(ip_train, op_train), (ip_test, op_test) = data.load_data()
```

Step 3: Check the shape of the images.

This displays the shape of the training and test input data.

```
print(ip_train.shape, ip_test.shape)
```

As we can see, it has three dimensions here: the number of images in the set, the width, and the height.

Step 4: Reshape the input values.

Usually, we have datasets with images that are colored. This means that all three RGB (Red Green Blue) channels are available. Now in TensorFlow, an image that is fully colored has a depth of 3. However, the Fashion MNIST dataset consists of greyscale images, which means it is just black and white. Thus, it has a depth of 1.

In this step, we reshape the images from having a dimension of (n, width, height) to having a new dimension of (n, width, height, depth), where *n* is the number of images in the set.

The code will look like this:

```
ip_train = ip_train.reshape((60000, 28, 28, 1))
ip_test = ip_test.reshape((10000, 28, 28, 1))

print(ip_train.shape, ip_train.shape)
```

Now when we display the reshaped data, it will show four dimensions.

Step 5: Prepare the data.

Once again, we need to normalize the data, as shown here:

```
ip_train, ip_test = ip_train / 255.0, ip_test / 255.0
```

Step 6: Build the neural network.

This time, we will add two extra dense layers to our neural network, with 128 and 1,000 neurons in them respectively, and each having the activation function ReLu. We will also add an extra "dropout layer" before the final layer, which helps to prevent overfitting.

```
model = models.Sequential([
    layers.Flatten(input_shape=(28, 28, 1)),
    layers.Dense(128, activation='relu'),
    layers.Dense(1000, activation='relu'),
    layers.Dropout(0.5),
    layers.Dense(10, activation='softmax')
])
```

Step 7: Compile the model.

Before fitting the model, we compile the model, like this:

```
model.compile(optimizer = 'adam',
                    loss = 'sparse_categorical_
                    crossentropy',
                    metrics = ['accuracy'])
```

Step 8: View the model.

```
model.summary()
```

We will get the summary of the model, like in Figure 11-10.

In [11]: model.summary()

Model: "sequential"

Layer (type)	Output Shape	Param #
flatten (Flatten)	(None, 784)	0
dense (Dense)	(None, 128)	100480
dense_1 (Dense)	(None, 1000)	129000
dropout (Dropout)	(None, 1000)	0
dense_2 (Dense)	(None, 10)	10010

Total params: 239,490
Trainable params: 239,490
Non-trainable params: 0

Figure 11-10. *Summary of the model*

Step 9: Train the model.

```
model.fit(ip_train, op_train, epochs = 5)
```

The model will begin training through five epochs, as shown in Figure 11-11.

```
In [14]: model.fit(ip_train, op_train, epochs = 5)
         Train on 60000 samples
         Epoch 1/5
         60000/60000 [==============================] - 6s 107us/sample - loss: 0.3024 - accuracy: 0.8876
         Epoch 2/5
         60000/60000 [==============================] - 6s 103us/sample - loss: 0.2915 - accuracy: 0.8924
         Epoch 3/5
         60000/60000 [==============================] - 6s 100us/sample - loss: 0.2812 - accuracy: 0.8962
         Epoch 4/5
         60000/60000 [==============================] - 6s 101us/sample - loss: 0.2714 - accuracy: 0.8989
         Epoch 5/5
         60000/60000 [==============================] - 6s 101us/sample - loss: 0.2654 - accuracy: 0.9008
Out[14]: <tensorflow.python.keras.callbacks.History at 0x14de06e50>
```

Figure 11-11. *Training the model through five epochs*

Step 10: Test the model.

In this step, we will use something called verbose.

The verbose *command is used to provide information about a particular task.*

We can alter the amount of information that we get by setting verbose at either 1 or 2.

At 0, we get nothing.

At 1, we get a progress bar and the number of epochs, along with the loss and accuracy.

At 2, we get only the number of epochs along with the loss and accuracy, without the progress bar.

```
model.evaluate(ip_test, op_test, verbose = 2)
```

We will obtain an output as shown in Figure 11-12.

```
In [17]:  model.evaluate(ip_test, op_test, verbose = 2)
          10000/10000 - 0s - loss: 0.3671 - accuracy: 0.8706
Out[17]:  [0.3670895663022995, 0.8706]
```

Figure 11-12. *Evaluating the model*

Step 11: Carry out inference.

First, we need to define a list in which we mention the class names, since these are not given in the dataset. The list can be found on the TensorFlow website.

We create the list like this:

```
class_names = ['T-shirt/top', 'Trouser', 'Pullover', 'Dress',
'Coat', 'Sandal', 'Shirt', 'Sneaker', 'Bag', 'Ankle boot']
```

Following the same code as before, we can check the accuracy of our model

```
:import matplotlib.pyplot as plt
%matplotlib inline

test_image=ip_test[5000]

plt.imshow(test_image.reshape(28,28))
```

This will give us the test image shown in Figure 11-13.

In [69]:

Out[69]: `<matplotlib.image.AxesImage at 0x13d61dc50>`

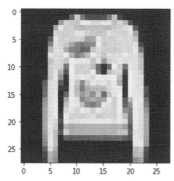

Figure 11-13. *The test image*

We can now proceed to convert the image into a NumPy array, reshape it, pass it through our model, and obtain a prediction.

```
import numpy as np

from tensorflow.keras.preprocessing import image

test_image = image.img_to_array(test_image)

test_image = test_image.reshape(1, 28, 28, 1)

result = model.predict(test_image)
result

np.around(result)

n=(np.around(result)).argmax()
print(n)
```

This gives us the following output:

2

This output is very vague. All it tells us is the position of the predicted class, but not what the actual item of clothing is. Thus, we add an extra line of code:

```
print(class_names[n])
```

This will give us the following output:

```
Pullover
```

In this way, we print the value at the *n*th position of the list, which in this case is "Pullover."

So, there we have it! We have built our very first multi-layer neural network that can classify images with an accuracy of close to 90 percent.

Task Time   We have just completed building two neural networks that can carry out multi-class image classification. One of them is a single-layer neural network, while the other is multi-layered. Can you try interchanging the datasets to see how the model's accuracy changes based on the number of layers? And, once you have done that, try changing the number of layers, as well as the number of epochs. What's the highest accuracy you are able to achieve?

We will now move forward to a very interesting concept that we learned about in the beginning of the book, which is convolutional neural networks.

As you might remember, CNNs use convolution layers and pooling layers to process the given data. The great thing about them is that they can process 2D images and detect important features very easily. This is why they are frequently used with image classification problems.

Let's have a look at some convolutional neural networks to see how well they work for image classification.

Program 4: Clothing Classification Using Convolutional Neural Networks (Multi-layer, Multi-class)

The structure for this model is similar to the previous ones. The only major difference is that the neural network will now have convolution layers and pooling layers.

The Structure

Here is how the CNN model works for image classification:

1. It loads the given dataset of images.

2. It divides the data into the training set and the test set.

3. It creates the convolutional neural network with as many layers as we specify, along with the activation function provided by us.

4. It also creates the last dense layer and the output layer with the parameters provided by us.

5. It then begins training with the training data to recognize the similarities and differences between each image and segregate them accordingly.

6. Finally, it tests its accuracy with the test data to see how well it has learned the differences between each image.

Dataset

The dataset that we will be using for this program is the Fashion MNIST dataset.

API

We will be using the Keras API within TensorFlow.

The Activation Functions

We will be using two activation functions here:

1. ReLU

2. Softmax

The Optimizer

We will be using the Adam optimizer in this neural network.

The Program

Step 1: Import the TensorFlow library and Keras utilities.

```
import tensorflow as tf

from tensorflow.keras import datasets, layers, models
```

Step 2: Load the Fashion MNIST dataset.

```
data = datasets.fashion_mnist
(ip_train, op_train), (ip_test, op_test) = data.load_data()
```

Step 3: Check the shape of the images.

```
print(ip_train.shape, ip_test.shape)
```

Step 4: Reshape the input values.

```
ip_train = ip_train.reshape((60000, 28, 28, 1))
ip_test = ip_test.reshape((10000, 28, 28, 1))

print(ip_train.shape, ip_test.shape)
```

Now when we display the reshaped data, it will show four dimensions.

Step 5: Prepare the data.

Once again, we must normalize the data by dividing it by 255.

```
ip_train, ip_test = ip_train / 255.0, ip_test / 255.0
```

Step 6: Build the convolutional neural network.

Here is where the main difference comes in. Since we are making a CNN model, the neural network will require convolution layers and pooling layers.

```
model=models.Sequential()
model.add(layers.Conv2D(32,(3,3),activation="relu",input_shape=(28,28,1)))
model.add(layers.MaxPooling2D((2,2)))
model.add(layers.Conv2D(64,(3,3), activation="relu"))
model.add(layers.MaxPooling2D((2,2)))
model.add(layers.Conv2D(64,(3,3), activation="relu"))
```

As you can see, we have three convolution layers and two max pooling layers. We use the ReLU activation function for all the convolution layers. There is also no need to flatten the images before feeding them to the model, as CNNs can process two-dimensional data. This is why we use Conv2D instead of Conv1D.

The first convolution layer consists of 32 filters or kernels, each of size 3x3. The output from this layer gets passed on to the pooling layer with a filter of size 2x2. Likewise, the output gets transferred to each successive layer, until it reaches the last convolution layer.

Step 7: Add the final dense layer and output layer.

We must now add the last fully connected layer, followed by the output layer. Here, we need to flatten the input first before feeding it to the dense layer.

The dense layer will have the ReLU activation function and 64 neurons.

The last layer here is called the classification layer. It uses a Softmax activation function and will have ten neurons, corresponding to the number of outputs or classes that we will obtain.

```
model.add(layers.Flatten())
model.add(layers.Dense(64, activation='relu'))
model.add(layers.Dense(10, activation='softmax'))
```

Step 8: Compile the model.

```
model.compile(optimizer = 'adam',
                         loss = 'sparse_categorical_
                         crossentropy',
                         metrics = ['accuracy'])
```

Step 9: View the model.

```
model.summary()
```

We will get the summary of the CNN model, as shown in Figure 11-14.

```
In [11]:  model.summary()

          Model: "sequential"
          _____
          Layer (type)                 Output Shape              Param #
          =================================================================
          conv2d (Conv2D)              (None, 26, 26, 32)        320
          _____
          max_pooling2d (MaxPooling2D) (None, 13, 13, 32)        0
          _____
          conv2d_1 (Conv2D)            (None, 11, 11, 64)        18496
          _____
          max_pooling2d_1 (MaxPooling2 (None, 5, 5, 64)          0
          _____
          conv2d_2 (Conv2D)            (None, 3, 3, 64)          36928
          _____
          flatten (Flatten)            (None, 576)               0
          _____
          dense (Dense)                (None, 64)                36928
          _____
          dense_1 (Dense)              (None, 10)                650
          =================================================================
          Total params: 93,322
          Trainable params: 93,322
          Non-trainable params: 0
          _____
```

Figure 11-14. *Summary of the CNN model*

Step 10: Train the model.

```
model.fit(ip_train, op_train, epochs = 5)
```

This will begin training the model through five epochs, as shown in Figure 11-15.

```
In [12]:  model.fit(ip_train, op_train, epochs = 5)

          Train on 60000 samples
          Epoch 1/5
          60000/60000 [==============================] - 43s 725us/sample - loss: 0.5001 - accuracy: 0.8179
          Epoch 2/5
          60000/60000 [==============================] - 44s 741us/sample - loss: 0.3245 - accuracy: 0.8809
          Epoch 3/5
          60000/60000 [==============================] - 45s 754us/sample - loss: 0.2802 - accuracy: 0.8970
          Epoch 4/5
          60000/60000 [==============================] - 45s 744us/sample - loss: 0.2476 - accuracy: 0.9095
          Epoch 5/5
          60000/60000 [==============================] - 49s 816us/sample - loss: 0.2247 - accuracy: 0.9165
Out[12]:  <tensorflow.python.keras.callbacks.History at 0x139ff4b90>
```

Figure 11-15. *Training the model*

Step 11: Test the model.

```
model.evaluate(ip_test, op_test, verbose = 1)
```

This will test the model to show its accuracy, as shown in Figure 11-16.

```
In [13]: model.evaluate(ip_test, op_test, verbose = 1)
         10000/10000 [==============================] - 2s 245us/sample - loss: 0.2603 - accuracy: 0.9055
Out[13]: [0.2603404054045677, 0.9055]
```

Figure 11-16. *Testing the CNN model*

There you have it! The image classification model using a convolutional neural network is now complete. You can play around with it to add or remove layers, and to change the parameters as well.

Let's take a look at another example of a CNN model.

Program 5: Handwriting Recognition Using Convolutional Neural Networks (Multi-layer, Multi-class)

The structure, API, activation functions, and optimizer will remain the same. However, we will try this program with another dataset. This time, we will also add the code for inference.

Dataset

The dataset that we will be using for this program is the regular MNIST dataset.

The Program

Step 1: Import the TensorFlow library and Keras utilities.

```
import tensorflow as tf

from tensorflow.keras import datasets, layers, models
```

Step 2: Load the MNIST dataset.

```
data = datasets.mnist
(ip_train, op_train), (ip_test, op_test) = data.load_data()
```

Step 3: Reshape the input values.

```
ip_train = ip_train.reshape((60000, 28, 28, 1))
ip_test = ip_test.reshape((10000, 28, 28, 1))

print(ip_train.shape, ip_test.shape)
```

Step 4: Prepare the data.

```
ip_train, ip_test = ip_train / 255.0, ip_test / 255.0
```

Step 6: Build the convolutional neural network.

Once again, we must add the convolution and max pooling layers.

```
model=models.Sequential()
model.add(layers.Conv2D(30,(3,3),activation="relu",input_shape=(28,28,1)))
model.add(layers.MaxPooling2D((2,2)))
model.add(layers.Conv2D(60,(3,3), activation="relu"))
model.add(layers.MaxPooling2D((2,2)))
model.add(layers.Conv2D(90,(3,3), activation="relu"))
```

Step 7: Add the final dense layer, dropout layer, and output layer.

```
model.add(layers.Flatten())
model.add(layers.Dense(64, activation='relu'))
model.add(layers.Dropout(0.5))
model.add(layers.Dense(10, activation='softmax'))
```

Step 8: Compile the model.

```
model.compile(optimizer = 'adam',
                        loss = 'sparse_categorical_crossentropy',
                        metrics = ['accuracy'])
```

Step 9: View the model.

```
model.summary()
```

Step 10: Train the model.

```
model.fit(ip_train, op_train, epochs = 5)
```

Step 11: Test the model.

```
model.evaluate(ip_test, op_test, verbose = 1)
```

Step 12: Carry out inference.

Import the Matplotlib library into the Jupyter notebook like this:

```
import matplotlib.pyplot as plt
%matplotlib inline
```

Select the test image:

```
test_image=ip_test[180]
```

Plot the image:

```
plt.imshow(test_image.reshape(28,28))
```

We will get the image shown in Figure 11-17.

```
In [27]:  plt.imshow(test_image.reshape(28,28))
Out[27]:  <matplotlib.image.AxesImage at 0x13b57d610>
```

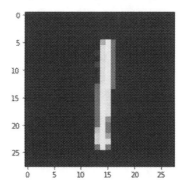

Figure 11-17. *Plotting the image*

Import the Numpy library and the image function under Keras:

```
import numpy as np
```

```
from tensorflow.keras.preprocessing import image
```

Convert the test image into an array and reshape it:

```
test_image = image.img_to_array(test_image)
test_image = test_image.reshape(1,28,28,1)
```

Allow the model to predict the class of the image:

```
result = model.predict(test_image)
result
```

Round off the results and find the maximum value among them:

```
np.around(result)
```

```
(np.around(result)).argmax()
```

We will get the output as 1. This shows that the model has correctly predicted the class of the image.

There we have it! Our second CNN model is now complete. By changing the parameters, we can play around with it to see how high the accuracy can get.

Now, let's try one last program just to challenge ourselves. This time, we will use a brand new dataset; i.e., CIFAR-10.

Program 6: Image Classification for CIFAR-10 Using Convolutional Neural Networks (Multi-layer, Multi-class)

Before we begin this program, let's have a look at the dataset that we will be working with.

The Dataset

The dataset that we will be using in this program is CIFAR-10, which stands for Canadian Institute For Advanced Research. It is a collection of 60,000 color images, each of size 32x32. There are ten different classes, with 6,000 images within each class. There are 50,000 training images and 10,000 test images.

The ten different classes are airplanes, cars, birds, cats, deer, dogs, frogs, horses, ships, and trucks. Researchers can quickly train machine learning and computer vision models with the help of this dataset.

Everything else is similar to the previous CNN programs, so let's just go ahead with the program. Since by now the different steps involved in creating the model should be clear, we need not go through this program step-by-step. We will directly type in each line of code.

The Program

Let's start by writing the code to build, train, and test the model, as follows:

```python
import tensorflow as tf

from tensorflow.keras import datasets, layers, models

from tensorflow.keras.datasets import cifar10

(ip_train, op_train), (ip_test, op_test) = cifar10.load_data()

print(ip_train.shape, ip_test.shape)

ip_train = ip_train.reshape(ip_train.shape[0], 32, 32, 3)
ip_test = ip_test.reshape(ip_test.shape[0], 32, 32, 3)

ip_train, ip_test = ip_train / 255.0, ip_test / 255.0

model=models.Sequential()
model.add(layers.Conv2D(32,(3,3),activation="relu",input_shape=(32,32,3)))
model.add(layers.MaxPooling2D((2,2)))
model.add(layers.Conv2D(64,(3,3), activation="relu"))
model.add(layers.MaxPooling2D((2,2)))
model.add(layers.Conv2D(64,(3,3), activation="relu"))

model.add(layers.Flatten())
model.add(layers.Dense(64, activation='relu'))
model.add(layers.Dense(10, activation='softmax'))

model.compile(optimizer = 'adam',
                    loss = 'sparse_categorical_crossentropy',
                    metrics = ['accuracy'])

model.summary()

model.fit(ip_train, op_train, epochs = 10)

model.evaluate(ip_test, op_test, verbose = 2)
```

Now let's write the code for inference:

```
import matplotlib.pyplot as plt
%matplotlib inline

test_image=ip_test[20]
```

Remember, the number within the square brackets can be changed accordingly, to select different test images.

```
plt.imshow(test_image.reshape(32,32,3))

import numpy as np

from tensorflow.keras.preprocessing import image

classes = ["airplane", "automobile", "bird", "cat", "deer",
"dog", "frog", "horse", "ship", "truck"]

test_image = image.img_to_array(test_image)
test_image = test_image.reshape(1,32,32,3)

result = model.predict(test_image)
result

np.around(result)

n=(np.around(result)).argmax()

print(classes[n])
```

When I ran the inference, I got two different outcomes:

- The first test image was that of a horse, and the model was able to correctly identify the image.

- The second image was that of a bird, but the model classified it as an airplane instead.

Try changing the test image and then carry out inference. Are you able to get an accurate prediction?

Task Time   You can find some great open source datasets online that you can easily download and use for non-commercial purposes. Try getting some new datasets and load them into your Jupyter notebook. Then, create a deep learning CNN model to classify the images. Keep playing around with the parameters, add or remove layers, and see how accurate you can make it!

Most deep learning models are used for multi-class classification. However, what if there were a need for binary classification, in which there are only two classes? Usually, these kinds of models are used for problems where the answer is either "yes" or "no." For example:

- Is the motorist wearing a helmet?
- Is the light bulb on?
- Is the email spam?

That said, let's go through a program in which we will carry out binary classification using convolutional neural networks. The dataset that we will be using is the "Dogs vs. Cats" dataset from Kaggle.

Program 7: Dogs vs. Cats Classification Using Convolutional Neural Networks (Multi-layer, Binary)

In this program, we will train the model to differentiate between a dog and a cat. This seems like a trivial task for the human brain, but for the machine, it may not be so easy. Remember in Program 1, where we used two pre-trained models and carried out inference on the image of a kitten?

For the first image, they identified it correctly as an Egyptian Cat. For the second image, however, one predicted that the image was that of a Chihuahua, while the other said that it was a Pembroke Welsh Corgi.

The reason for this is probably because all three breeds have pointed ears and small features. Although this doesn't make much of a difference to us, it does make a huge impact on an artificially intelligent machine, because every little feature is important for a deep learning model's learning process.

Let's have a look at our dataset.

The Dataset

The "Dogs vs. Cats" dataset can be found on the Kaggle website. It consists of a total of 25,000 images of dogs and cats. Although we do not know how the images are separated out initially, we will find this out during the program.

The Program

Step 1: Import all the required libraries and functions into Jupyter Notebook.

```
import tensorflow as tf

from tensorflow.keras.models import Sequential
from tensorflow.keras.layers import Conv2D
from tensorflow.keras.layers import MaxPooling2D
from tensorflow.keras.layers import Flatten
from tensorflow.keras.layers import Dense

import os
```

The os module allows users to interact with the operating system.

This time, we will create our model first, after which we will download the dataset.

Step 2: Develop the CNN model and compile it.

Here, we refer to our model as classifier. We can put any name we want, provided it is easily understood by anyone who reads it.

```
classifier = Sequential()

classifier.add(Conv2D(64,(3,3),input_shape = (64,64,3),
activation = 'relu'))

classifier.add(MaxPooling2D(pool_size = (2,2)))

classifier.add(Conv2D(64,(3,3), activation = 'relu'))
classifier.add(MaxPooling2D(pool_size = (2,2)))

classifier.add(Conv2D(64,(3,3), activation = 'relu'))
classifier.add(MaxPooling2D(pool_size = (2,2)))

classifier.add(Flatten())

classifier.add(Dense(units = 128, activation = 'relu'))
classifier.add(Dense(units = 1, activation = 'sigmoid'))

classifier.compile(optimizer='adam',loss='binary_crossentropy',metrics=
['accuracy'])
```

Step 3: Transform the imported data.

```
from tensorflow.keras.preprocessing.image import
ImageDataGenerator

train_datagen = ImageDataGenerator(
        rescale=1./255,
        shear_range=0.2,
        zoom_range=0.2,
        horizontal_flip=True)

test_datagen = ImageDataGenerator(rescale=1./255)
```

Step 4: Download the dataset.

The dataset needs to be downloaded from a specific link. In this section of code, we tell our program to download the data from the given url, and then we store it on our system.

```
_URL = 'https://storage.googleapis.com/mledu-datasets/cats_and_
dogs_filtered.zip'

path_to_zip = tf.keras.utils.get_file('cats_and_dogs.zip',
origin=_URL, extract=True)


PATH=os.path.join(os.path.dirname(path_to_zip),'cats_and_dogs_filtered')
```

Step 5: Set up the directories.

We need to set up different directories for the training and testing data, and then separate out the cat and dog images accordingly.

```
trainingdir = os.path.join(data_path, 'train')
testingdir = os.path.join(data_path, 'validation')

# directory with the training cat pictures
cats_train = os.path.join(trainingdir, 'cats')

# directory with the training dog pictures
dogs_train = os.path.join(trainingdir, 'dogs')

# directory with the testing cat pictures
cats_test = os.path.join(testingdir, 'cats')

# directory with the testing dog pictures
dogs_test = os.path.join(testingdir, 'dogs')
```

Step 6: Find the number of elements in each directory.

We first find the number of elements directories in each directory, and then we display the values.

```
cats_train_num = len(os.listdir(cats_train))
dogs_train_num = len(os.listdir(dogs_train))

cats_test_num = len(os.listdir(cats_test))
dogs_test_num = len(os.listdir(dogs_test))

train_tot = cats_train_num + dogs_train_num
test_tot = cats_test_num + dogs_test_num

print(cats_train_num)
print(dogs_train_num)

print(cats_test_num)
print(dogs_test_num)

print(train_tot)
print(test_tot)
```

We should get output like this:

```
1000

1000

500

500

2000

1000
```

Step 7: Load the training data and testing data, and display the label map.

We load the training and testing images directories, and add the batch size, target size, and class mode as needed. Here, we set the batch size to be 128, and the target size to be 64x64.

For the training data:

```
train_data = train_datagen.flow_from_directory(batch_size=128,
                                        directory=trainingdir,
                                         target_size=(64, 64),
                                         class_mode='binary')
```

This will give an output like this:

```
Found 2000 images belonging to 2 classes.
```

For the testing data:

```
test_data = test_datagen.flow_from_directory(batch_size=128,
                                        directory=testingdir,
                                        target_size=(64, 64),
                                        class_mode='binary')
```

This will give an output like this:

```
Found 1000 images belonging to 2 classes.
```

We then display the numerical identities of the two classes, as shown here:

```
label_map = (train_data.class_indices)
print(label_map)
```

This gives us an output like this:

```
{'cats': 0, 'dogs': 1}
```

Thus, 0 refers to the cats class, while 1 refers to the dogs class.

Step 8: Train the model.

We can now start training our model. We will run it through thirty epochs this time:

```
classifier.fit(
        train_data,
        epochs=30,
        validation_data=test_data)
```

After thirty epochs, I got a validation accuracy of 77 percent. You can try changing the number of epochs to see if that has any significant effect on your model.

Once the model is done training, we can carry out inference and see how well the model works.

Step 9: Carry out inference.

For this process, we will use two pictures of our own: one of a cat and one of a dog.

We will begin by importing the necessary packages, as follows:

```
import numpy as np
from tensorflow.keras.preprocessing import image
```

Now, let us load our images into our program. The images have already been saved in the same folder as the program, so there is no need to add the entire file path. Just the file's name shall suffice.

```
test_image_1= image.load_img('Dog.jpeg', target_size = (64,64))
test_image_2= image.load_img('Cat.jpeg', target_size = (64,64))
```

We can then display the test images separately, as shown in Figure 11-18 and Figure 11-19.

test_image_1

Figure 11-18. *A dog image*

test_image_2

Figure 11-19. *A cat image*

We now type in the rest of the code, as follows:

```
test_image_1 = image.img_to_array(test_image_1)

test_image_2 = image.img_to_array(test_image_2)

test_image_1 = test_image_1.reshape(1,64,64,3)
test_image_2 = test_image_2.reshape(1,64,64,3)

result1 = model.predict(test_image_1)
result2 = model.predict(test_image_2)

print(result1, result2)
```

Now, to print the predictions we type in the following code for the first image:

```
if result1 == 1:
    prediction1 = 'dog'
else:
    prediction1 = 'cat'

print(prediction1)
```

This gives the following output:

```
'dog'
```

Now when we run the following code:

```
if result2 == 1:
    prediction2 = 'dog'
else:
    n2 = 'cat'

print(prediction2)
```

We get the following output:

```
'cat'
```

And that's it! The binary neural network is ready. We can keep altering different parts of the code to increase the accuracy until we reach a result that is satisfactory.

Note   In some cases, you may also need to install the "pillow" library (Python Imaging Library, abbreviated as "PIL"), as this provides support to work with images of various formats. It's easy to install it using `pip`: `pip install pillow`

The great thing about these machine learning models is that the structure pretty much remains the same for all types of data. What we need to know is how to prepare and manipulate the data before feeding it to the model. As we try out these programs on our own, with different datasets and modified input layers and values, the entire process will become much easier to do. Just don't forget to consistently practice, as this will help you to improve your skills and become proficient in what you do.

Summary

In this chapter, we learned all about how we can build, train, and validate our deep learning models using TensorFlow and the Keras API, all with the help of Jupyter Notebook. We understood the general structure of a working machine learning model, and we also got better acquainted with Keras. We then differentiated between the types of classification problems—binary and multi-class—and had a quick introduction to image classification. Finally, we wrote seven different programs to enhance what we have learned so far, of which one program involved a pre-trained model, one program included binary classification, one program was single layered, and the rest of the programs carried out multi-layer multi-class classification.

These programs are a great start for anyone who is new to the world of TensorFlow 2.0. Don't worry if you aren't able to understand them immediately. As you keep playing around with them on your own, they will make much more sense to you. You can use these models as a starting point to develop your own neural networks for different datasets. And, once you get more and more comfortable with programming, you can begin adding your own changes to them to create even more professional models.

Quick Links

The MNIST dataset: `http://yann.lecun.com/exdb/mnist/`

The Fashion MNIST dataset: `https://github.com/zalandoresearch/fashion-mnist`

The CIFAR-10 dataset: `https://www.cs.toronto.edu/~kriz/cifar.html`

The Dogs vs. Cats dataset: `https://www.kaggle.com/c/dogs-vs-cats/data`

About Keras: `https://keras.io/`

Keras optimizers: `https://keras.io/optimizers/`

Conclusion

In this book, we started by learning what Artificial Intelligence, Machine Learning, and Deep Learning are. We saw their applications and went through their important concepts. We also compared Machine Learning with Deep Learning to find out exactly how they differ even though the latter is a subset of the former.

We then came to know about the different platforms that we can use to program, and had a look at their varying features. This led us to the Jupyter Notebook application. We learned what it is, why it is recommended to be used instead of a text editor or a regular IDE, and what its advantages and disadvantages are. We also explored its features and practiced using it for some basic Python programming techniques.

After this, we were introduced to TensorFlow, which is a very important Machine Learning library in Python. We saw how it has worked so far, and studied its pros and cons. We even went through its features as we had a look at some simple Python programming using TensorFlow 1.0.

Finally, we learned about TensorFlow 2.0. We studied its updates and changes, how it varies from its parent version, and how our old TensorFlow 1.0 code can be converted into TensorFlow 2.0 code. We compared features, as well as coding syntax. We even developed some Machine Learning models with the help of TensorFlow, which included regular Neural Networks and Convolutional Neural Networks. These models were trained with some data, validated, and then used for inference.

The overall aim of this book is to help AI enthusiasts, especially beginners, to learn how to code in Python, using TensorFlow 2.0, with the help of the Jupyter Notebook. It's a three in one package, as you gain the knowledge of a popular programming language, a powerful Machine

© Nikita Silaparasetty 2020
N. Silaparasetty, *Machine Learning Concepts with Python
and the Jupyter Notebook Environment*, https://doi.org/10.1007/978-1-4842-5967-2

CONCLUSION

Learning library within that language, and a convenient interface that allows you to write working code on it. The programs in the last chapter are also intended to boost your understanding to a greater extent. By the time you complete this book, you should feel confident enough to pursue higher levels within the field of Artificial Intelligence. You can even go ahead and share the knowledge that you have gained with others!

Since its conception, Artificial Intelligence has always been an area that is looked at with great optimism and enthusiasm. Despite the few minor hitches here and there, it has proven its worth through its many successful applications. AI enthusiasts continue to remain motivated, especially in these modern times, where technology has vastly improved, allowing AI to be used to a greater extent.

The importance of Artificial Intelligence is rapidly spreading out and reaching more and more people, and many are expanding their knowledge of this area in order to jump on the bandwagon. This can have both positive and negative consequences - Positive, because there is more workforce available in the area; Negative, because there might be too much competition but less expertise. With the right skilled labour, better AI can be developed, and many more implementations can be introduced.

Artificial Intelligence is a never-ending topic of interest. Once we take a step into it, we cannot just take a step out and walk away. The whole concept of creating machines that can think and respond like human beings has and will continue to intrigue the human mind. There doesn't seem to be any chance of putting an end to its research and development in the near or distant future, making it one of the most highly-demanded fields, in terms of study as well as employment.

There are still many questions that are yet to be answered -

Will it lead to a state of utopia or dystopia?

Will it ever completely replace manual labour with machine-delivered work?

Will there ever be robots that can perfectly think, act, behave, and express like human beings?

Will there ever be a point at which AI just cannot be improved further?
Can AI become powerful enough to take over the world?

Apart from making interesting plots for science-fiction stories, questions like these can also provide us with interesting insights that can help us to improve the integration of AI in the future. Ultimately, even if Artificial Intelligence becomes powerful enough to simulate living beings, nothing can truly replace the natural intelligence that only human beings are blessed with. It is up to us, how we build and develop our machines. Thus, by ensuring the proper use of our resources, efforts, and of course, our natural intelligence, as well as by keeping good intentions and objectives in mind, we can successfully produce groundbreaking artificially intelligent technology that can improve our standard of living and radically transform our everyday life.

Index

Printed in the United States
By Bookmasters